Everyone's a
Storyteller

Inventive ☉ Imaginative ☉ Innovative Storytelling

by eileen hoard

The author grants permission for the copying
of the following pages for personal use:

39-51; 58-62; 104-110; 113-119;
136-140; 144-145; 168-169

ISBN: 0-9759519-0-4

Library of Congress Control Number: 200409501

Printed by:

Thomas G. Treiber, CFC, CCG

Specialized Office Systems, Inc.
Bruce Goldberg, President
Phoenix, Arizona 85024
800-234-5767
email: tom@SOSsystems.com
www.SOSsystems.com

All photos were taken by Robin Damore,
photographer and portrait artist

Cover illustration by Amy Rogers

Cover and book Design by Ronda Johnson

Orders: Eileen Hoard • 602-943-6117

See the website: www.everyonesastoryteller.com

This book is dedicated to my husband, Bob,

who always encourages me to do my 'thing.'

Once you realize that you can't do it all…you find there are many talented people in your life who will willingly help you. I owe a huge thank you to:

Marilyn Rampley, preschool partner and forever friend who initiated the publishing process, read copy and offered suggestions.

Kristen Hoard, daughter and computer guru who organized my ideas and set up my web site.

My handsome husband, Bob, who always encourages me to do my 'thing'.

Dr. Cindy Hoard, daughter, psychologist and computer whiz, who spent long hours at the computer and gently offered editing advice. She ended up doing so much more than either of us anticipated.

Michelle Schwartz, daughter, marketing entrepreneur, and a trainer, who offered strategies and ideas.

Robin Damore, daughter, photographer and portrait artist, who dropped everything to shoot photos for this book.

Many, many thanks to Ronda Johnson for getting the book "back on track".

Grandchildren: Andrea, Madeline, Maxine and Cassidy for their stories.
A talented, persistent editor, Debbie Moyer, who became a friend.
Also "Thank You" to the many children and teachers who have
- *listened,*
- *laughed,*
- *shared ideas and*
- *participated*

in storytelling sessions over the years. I have learned from all of you.

You have been my teachers.

All patterns may be enlarged to 8.5 X 11 or to meet your needs.

EVERYONE'S A STORYTELLER

WHAT YOU WILL FIND IN THIS BOOK...

EVERYONE'S A STORYTELLER

ADULT RESOURCES, PICTURE BOOKS & TRADITIONAL TALES & RHYMES

EVERYONE'S A STORYTELLER

This book is for all of our children. It is also for all moms, dads, nanas, papas, nannies and teachers. All are storytellers...and all are teachers. This book is also for all, who, over the years, have taught history, wisdom and culture through storytelling.

INTRODUCTION

- First premise...ANYBODY can be a storyteller.
- Second premise...EVERYONE is a storyteller already!

Every day we tell some silly, clever or funny story about our friends, children or spouse. We ask, How was your operation? What happened the day you had the baby?" We invite the story. "The automobile accident must have been terrible. Tell me about the day your house caught on fire. Was the wedding great? What is your most embarrassing memory?" So, don't tell me you're not a storyteller! Man, woman or child, we all tell stories all day long. We just don't realize it. Telling stories to a group of children may come as a challenge but gradually, if you so desire, you can come to the point where you realize that you are a storyteller. It took me more than two years of telling stories to children to say aloud, "I am a storyteller."

You have, no doubt, known some great natural storytellers. Men are notorious for telling yarns about hunting and fishing. Around a campfire, ghost stories abound. Grandmas and grandpas often share memories of their past. As adventurers and explorers spin tales we join them. As you listen to these stories, are you entranced? Many novelists describe themselves as storytellers. As everyday people, we too are storytellers.

In workshops I lead, I often ask each participant to tell a quick story to a partner. I ask them to choose something that happened to them recently. Maybe something endearing their own child or grandchild did, the neat comment of a student, or some loving or exasperating act of their partner. The room buzzes with voices. Everyone is eager to talk. That is when realization occurs: **Everybody has a story just waiting to be told.** As I work to quiet the group I can *authentically* point out *that they are storytellers!* Then I remind them it took me a couple of years to confidently say, "I am a storyteller."

Children have taught me much about telling a story. Some specifics include:
- Telling us a story will not necessarily be easy.
- You better use words we can understand.
- It's important to be **_very well prepared_**. We won't wait for you "to get it together."
- We will want to help you if you drop anything!
- You can grab our attention using your eyes. Look us straight in the eye, especially if we are giving you a problem.
- If you forget an important part of the story, just stop and say, "Did I forget to tell you...?" (The next time you tell that story we may expect you to say the same thing!)
- We may remember, even a year later, that you told a certain story.
- To us you are a like a TV Star! Enjoy it!

Teachers have taught me some things too.
- If you don't use caution, you may be on your own.
- Don't let us leave you with a group of children you don't know.
- You don't know our rules about children leaving the room and you will not know where we are if you need us.

- If you are doing a participation or dramatized story, ask us to choose children with whom to work.
- There are many unknowns in a new group of kids.
- Scan your program for stories which might be problematic to particular children.

For example, some children have had scary life situations. Time for clearing such with the teacher is rarely available, so exercise your own sensitivity.

You will likely add to these lists.

Most of my storytelling experience has been with children eighteen months through third grade. It all began when I was touched by a magic wand that turned me into a storyteller overnight.

Well, sort of…

What actually happened was that I was a partner in the first children's bookshop in Phoenix, Arizona, Sunpath Children's Bookshop. We were initially housed in a very small shop. There were five partners, all of us were women. Two of the partners (Dee and Tammy) concentrated on bookkeeping. Rayne did all of the ordering. When we enlarged our shop we decided to begin a monthly storytelling session. Cindy and I, though not very experienced, were left to become the storytellers. The children were precious, bright eyed and very young (eighteen months to 2-1/2 year-old toddlers predominated). Their parents brought the children and stayed with them (not necessarily quietly). Since *we* were inexperienced *we* adjusted to them. Getting them to listen involved not only piqueing their curiosity, but sometimes offering cookies. The children sat on a big fur blanket in our courtyard while their parents sat at the edges of the blanket or stood near our large lavender Jacaranda tree *and talked*. I learned early to concentrate on the story and the kids and to ignore the chatty parents. We both learned much quickly since we had few choices. Once we dressed up to do The *Greedy Old Fat Man* and invited the children to act out the story with us. That was Cindy's idea and the children loved it!

One day a woman from California came in to the shop and told me about a felt hamburger she had seen. That day *Big Mac* was born. Later, I wanted to tell *The Mitten*, so I made a big yellow felt mitten held together with Velcro and added cardboard animals wrapped with yarn. Ideas like this were born of necessity and monthly program demands.

That is how some of the ideas in this book were born, but many came later as I continued telling stories. While working and storytelling in the bookshop, I also served as Director of Shadow Rock Preschool where I often told stories in the classrooms. As preschool parents found their children entering public school I began to get calls to do Young Author Days for the early grades. I tried out my ideas there too. And so, my storytelling life continued.

Hopefully, the ideas in this book will be a good place for you to start your own storytelling experience. You can expand on existing material and experiment with creating new stories of your own. There is actually very little in print that covers telling stories to the very young.

I hope you will find these ideas useful as you delight young listeners with the magic of **your** storytelling.

An art as old as the human race, storytelling has never really been lost, but its spirit seems to have been slumbering for a while.
- Jimmy Neil Smith
National Association for the Preservation
And Perpetuation of Storytelling

In stories many things are true that aren't exactly true in real life.
- Jack Maguire

Stories have to be told or they die, and when they die, we can't remember who we are or why we're here.
- Sue Monk Kidd, Writer

Chapter 1
DEFINING STORYTELLING

• Definition of storytelling
• Who are storytellers
• You are a storyteller

I read a lot. A recent adult favorite of mine is Jean Auel's *Shelters of Stone*. For those of you unfamiliar with her series, *Earth's Children*, it is one set in prehistory. Her main character, Ayla, is a female finding her way among the caves and tribes of the period. Much research is evident in this book and I was taken with Auel's comments on the artistic qualities of storytelling and its place in the lives of early people. At one point Ayla, talking to Zelandoni, the first 'great storyteller,' asks her, "What do the words 'rhythm' and 'rhyme' mean?" Zelandoni replies, "Rhythm and rhyme help people to remember. Rhythm is the sense of movement. It carries you along as though you are walking at a steady pace. Rhymes are words that sound similar. They add to the rhythm, but they also help you remember the next words."

Later in the book Auel speaks eloquently about the meaning and value of storytelling:

> It wasn't only handicrafts that were valued. Entertainment was considered essential. Long, cold winters often kept people confined to their dwellings within the shelter for long periods of time, and they needed ways to alleviate the pressures of close quarters. Dancing and singing were enjoyed both as individual efforts and as community participation, and those who could play a flute well were as highly valued as those who made spears or baskets. Ayla had already learned that Story-Tellers were especially esteemed. Even the Clan, [the Neanderthals] had storytellers, Ayla recalled. They had particularly enjoyed the retelling of stories they knew.

> . . .Visitors were welcomed, if only because they usually brought new stories. They were urged to tell about their lives and adventures, whether or not they had dramatic narration skills, because it added a measure of interest and gave people something to discuss for long hours as they sat around winter fires. Although almost anyone could weave an interesting tale, those who showed a real talent for it were urged, coaxed and cajoled to pay visits to neighboring Caves which was the impetus that gave rise to the Traveling Story-Tellers. Some of them spent their lives, or at least several years, traveling from Cave to Cave, carrying news, bringing messages and telling stories. No one was more welcome.

> Most people could be quickly identified by designs on their clothing, and the necklaces or other jewelry that they wore, but over time the Story-Tellers had adopted a distinctive style of clothing and design that announced their profession. . . . Stories were often dramatized as well as narrated, but no matter how it was expressed, the Story and the Teller were always the focal point. (p. 489-490).[1]

Little wonder that, with such a long history, storytellers have taken their special place in each and every culture. I always find a minute in each presentation to reveal the importance storytellers have played in the nurturing and teaching of each generation. In the days before books and computers, TV and newspapers, storytelling was an important way to communicate. Even in the early years of the history of the United States when transportation was dangerous and slow, Presidents Jefferson, Madison and Adams relied on information from visitors who passed their homes to tell them the news.

Holding the attention of young children is always a challenge, but rarely will you find it easier and more successful than when you are engaged in telling stories. The children are intrigued because it is so up-close and personal. They don't know what you're going to do next and you have them hooked!

Whether you are telling real stories, fantasy or fable, you can charm an audience. One storyteller I know will only tell a tale that is true. She wants nothing to do with fantasy. This is the only way for her. Others spin tales totally made up of what might happen to real or imagined characters. Certainly another genre comprises humorous stories. Those usually have an unexpected twist at the end. Funny stories will always include some kind of a mix-up or joke. Mysteries are often specialty material aimed at older children and adults.

Many stories for young children are repetitive. They contain repeated lines or repeated actions. These are often described as cumulative stories in that the narrative is added to and all of the lines are repeated with each addition. *The Old Lady Who Swallowed a Fly* is, of course, a famous cumulative story.

Fairy tales are usually old stories which have knocked around the world so long that the identities of their authors are lost. You might be surprised, for example, to find out that many cultures have versions of *Cinderella* and, *Lazy Jack*. String stories like *The Mosquito* or *The Fly* are found in cultures from Japan to Africa. Just imagine sailors or their captains bringing stories home from their travels. They told these tales to their own children and often the stories changed a bit.

Stories may be used to teach. A teacher might dress as a well-known character and relate the facts of a portion of history. Consider acting out the day Edison finally developed a working light bulb. Think how that changed the world! Some movies or TV programs may tell us real stories too, although it is always interesting to wonder if they changed the facts to make the story more exciting. Of course, that could be an eye-opening assignment too — to discover how well history was preserved when a script was written.

At the preschool or elementary level, it is often possible to teach lessons with an appropriate story. With the help of that story, the teacher can hook the listeners into considering questions about behavior, feelings, consequences, and possibilities. The use of open-ended questions after a good story can create a learning experience. (Note: open-ended questions cannot be answered with yes or no. They demand that the child use expressive language and construct an answer using their own words, experiences and observations.)

Of course, storytelling as entertainment is probably its most common use. As adults, we are entertained constantly by stories on television and in movies and books. Even news shows tell us daily the story of what happened in our world. We talk on the telephone and tell each other our stories. We talk at dinner and want to hear the stories of the day from our families. We are **made** of stories. We **are** our stories.

Our whole life is about storytelling. Writers, songwriters, painters, sculptors, singers, actors, even religious leaders and teachers, often consider themselves to be storytellers. We cannot avoid it. We are all storytellers.

[1]Jean M. Auel, Shelters of Stone. (New York: Crown Publishers, 2002)

Inside each of us is a natural-born storyteller,
waiting to be released.

- Robin Moore, Storyteller and Author

If a child is to keep alive his inborn sense of wonder, he needs
the companionship of at least one adult who can share it,
rediscovering with him the joy, excitement, and mystery of the world we live in.

- Rachel Carson, Biologist and Writer

Chapter 2
HOW TO USE THIS BOOK

- If you are a parent, grandparent, aunt, uncle or friend…
- If you are a teacher…
- If you are a storyteller…
- If you are a nanny…

If you are a parent, grandparent, aunt, uncle or friend…

You may want to tell a story —

To calm…a familiar story may add to feelings of security or help children settle down at nap or bedtime.

To distract…to the three-year-old if a doll or toy is broken, the whole world is broken, but a story may divert catastrophic feelings.

To teach…you can teach opposites, for example, with *Mission Ziffoid* by Michael Rosen, or color with Eric Carle's *Mixed-Up Chameleon*. Identifying animals and animal sounds can be reinforced through storytelling. Some stories teach subtly. *Chicken Little* jumps to a conclusion while *The Little Red Hen* teaches helping.

To delight…you can entertain with drawn stories. Most drawn stories are short and children learn them rather easily. Soon they'll entertain their friends with them too. I can still remember my rather uncommunicative grandfather drawing the alphabet for me. "A" was always for apple, "B" was for ball, and "C" was drawn as a cat. It was always a treat!

To entertain…at home, waiting at the doctor's or dentist's office, waiting anywhere.

To promote thought…many traditional stories will trigger something to think about because they were written to teach morals and community values. Goldilocks didn't respect household and property. Dr. Seuss' *Horton Hatches the Egg* is about freedom and responsibility. *Swimmy* by Leo Lionni shows family and community working together for a common cause.

To get in touch with feelings…how did the character feel? And how would you feel?

To build memories…little tricks like *Flyaway Jack, Flyaway Jill* will be remembered long after the child has grown up.

As the parent you have an added attraction as a storyteller. Your children *always* want your undivided attention. The times you give it are times children treasure. Their reactions to a story may also give you an opening to talk with them about how they feel about similar happenings in their own lives. Storytelling can become a very cozy, special time to share with your children.

Many stories are good for laughs:
  Giraffe and a Half by Shel Silverstein
  Alligator Baby by Robert Munsch
  Old Black Fly by Jim Aylesworth
  Good Night Gorilla by Peggy Rathmann
  My Little Sister Ate One Hare by Bill Grossman
  I Know An Old Lady Who Swallowed a Pie by Alison Jackson
  No Way José by Joe Hayes
  Too Much Noise by Ann McGovern
  Click, Clack Moo, Cows That Type by Doreen Cronin
  Don't Make Me Laugh by James Stevenson

Some stories consider possibilities:
  It *Looked Like Spilt Milk* by Charles Shaw
      "It looked like an ice cream cone…, but it wasn't an ice cream cone."
  I'm Making a Pizza the Size of the Sun by Jack Prelutsky
      "My pizza is sure to be one of a kind."
  Cloudy with a Chance of Meatballs by Judith Barrett
      What if it did rain food?
  Just So Stories by Rudyard Kipling
      How the camel got his hump and the other explanations.

Some stories address familiar emotions:
  The Red Woolen Blanket by Bob Graham – getting along without a security blanket
  Pete's A Pizza by William Steig – changing moods
  Alligator Baby by Robert Munsch – getting a new baby
  Are You My Mother? by P.D. Eastman – being lost or separated from Mom

Stories wherein kids outsmart adults or giants:
  Jack and the Beanstalk – he finds the golden goose.
  The Emperor's New Clothes – the child speaks the truth.
  Jim and the Beanstalk – James helps the giant.
  Alligator Baby – big sister Kristen is smarter than Mom and Dad.

Stories in which kids act silly and do not think:
  Lazy Jack - a traditional tale about never getting it "right"
  Soap! Soap! Don't Forget the Soap! by Tom Birdseye – little boy who can not remember much
  Don't Forget the Bacon by Pat Hutchins – a forgetful boy

Stories that teach concepts:
  Nine in a Line by Ann Kirn – don't forget to count yourself
  The Doorbell Rang by Pat Hutchins – division of cookies and sharing
  Swimmy by Leo Lionni – acting as a community
  Fortunately by Remy Charlip – good news, bad news
  Little Blue, Little Yellow by Leo Lionni – how to make green
  It Looked Like Spilt Milk by Charles Shaw – shapes in the clouds
  Little Red Hen Traditional – value of helping

The Magic Spoon in *Jar of Fools* by Bill Gorah – was that magic?
The Lost Button by Arnold Lobel – friendship is a two way street.

You will enjoy going to the library to check out the previously listed books. Buy and keep the books that become your child's favorites. Before you know it, your children will be young adults or parents who cherish the books and stories you read to them in childhood. I read to my four girls all the time. I read favorites every day and poetry especially during scary Michigan lightning storms. Reading poetry while the lightning flashed seemed to calm my daughters. A handmade collection of poetry, a relic from my elementary teaching days, received tremendous use. I also owned a good book of poetry and simple stories which contained favorites of each daughter. Additionally, we owned individual picture books but since my children were young in the late 50's and 60's there were limited picture books. There were lots of Golden Books but we were just on the edge of the coming explosion of the children's books full of beautiful colorful illustrations. It was only thirty-five years ago that children enjoyed the quantity and quality of books similar to those available today.

When my first grandchild was born I was incredibly excited. She, *of course*, was the most beautiful baby. I could hardly wait to get my hands on her. As her parents came in the door from the hospital I reached for her. Her mom snatched her away asking, "Where is that book you always read to us? The big one, It's Mine, I want it!"

"Okay, all right, I'll get it," I said. "But first, give me that baby!"

We did begin reading to Andrea when she was only a few months old. Her favorite book was *Tales of Peter Rabbit.* When she was still a toddler and had very few words she would bring the little book to me and say, "Night, Night". She didn't want to go to sleep. She wanted me to open the book to the page which showed Mother Rabbit putting Peter down for a nap. She was reading the pictures in that book. This is an important step in the reading process and she began to do it early because she was constantly exposed to books and stories.

Each child's birth story is different and may be told and retold. The child will never tire of hearing it. What did Daddy say on the day I was born? What did Grandma forget and how did Grandpa sleep with me on his tummy? Mommy was busy holding me, feeding me, and changing my diapers. Older children also like to hear about what they did when they were little.

If you are eager to get started telling stories I suggest you try doing some of the drawn stories first. They are simple and easy to draw even if you are not artistic. You can write, so you can draw these stories which are circles, lines and easy shapes. Consider this… you are artistic. You have created your own signature. Banks and legal institutions recognize your identity by the signature you have designed. It has many of the same letters that other names have, perhaps even the very same letters, but the unique way in which your hand has created the lines sets it apart and proves **you are creative. Your signature proves…you are you**. You can draw on computer paper, a white board with dry erase pens, used envelopes, scrap paper, etc. Drawn stories are especially entertaining while waiting in doctors' offices with sick or cranky children. Once a child can draw circles and lines he/she can tell these stories too.

Perhaps you'll think of a story that you want to draw to add to your collection. Do it! Your kids will create some. Be sure to write down the words and preserve the drawings. Some day they can show them to their kids.

After library trips and drawn stories you may be quite ready to tackle nursery rhymes, fairy tales, or simple favorites of your family. Just jump in! Pick a story and learn it. Chapters four and five will give you some ideas about choosing and learning stories.

If public school teachers learn that you tell stories you will be in demand! You will certainly be a more animated reader but, of course, if you read aloud you are sure to hear, "I can't see the pictures!" I believe it is much more satisfying to TELL a story. You'll rarely hear, "I can't see..." when telling a story. If you do, simply remind the children to listen to the words and make the pictures in their minds.

At home you will also tell stories to get over the bumps that happen in all of our lives. You're on your way. Happy Storytelling!

If you are a teacher...

You already know what I know...
You can't teach anything if you don't have the child's attention!

That's why I began to create enhancements, or visuals, to capture the child's attention. Children are incredibly curious. I have often found that taking advantage of their curiosity gives me their attention in a spontaneous and positive way. They want to listen, so they do.

For example, sitting down with a paper bag, tote bag, large purse, small or large suitcase (if you have oversized stuff) creates instant curiosity and instant attention. If the "stuff" you are hiding changes all the time, they just don't know what you have in there! I hold the bag or container on my lap. Then, the discussion begins.

"What do you think I have in here? It could be a story or a caterpillar spinning a cocoon or a pile of shells to sort. Maybe it's a rock. What can you do that this beautiful rock cannot do?"

The class is thinking, engaged and learning. After they have all participated and you've thought together of many things you can do that the rock cannot do you might tell the story of *Sylvester and the Magic Pebble* by William Steig. You might use a wonderful Sylvester puppet which turns inside out to show the rock that Sylvester turned into one day when he was holding his magic pebble. The puppet helps to tell the story but you might also use a small red, glass pebble like Sylvester's to propel the story along. If the group is small enough you could give each of them a magic pebble of their own to help them remember the story. With the youngest it will also support the concept of the color red.

Getting the group's attention is key.

Any little token of any story that you can find or make to hold on your lap will help you maintain attention while you tell the story. The children can see your visual and they can see the story in their head. If the group is used to having books read to them they may actually say to you, "I can't see the pictures!" Then you might say, "Oh yes, you can. When I tell you a story you can see the pictures in your head!" They *can* see the pictures in their heads and they will.

In many cases you can find a story which will reinforce your concept for that day. Do not be too literal in choosing your story. Some examples include: *It Looked Like Spilt Milk* by Charles Shaw for clouds or *Little Blue, Little Yellow* by Leo Lionni for the concept green. Family stories abound as in *Alligator Baby* by Robert Munsch or the traditional *Goldilocks and the Three Bears.* I love *Fortunately* by Remy Charlip to accent positive and negative attitudes about the same subject. Self-image stories such as *I Like Me* and *Elmer* are also important. Of course, there are many more. The key is to look for connections which demonstrate the concept.

You are going to get an education in children's literature as you become a storyteller. What you already know will be a great help to you, but there are always new stories and books to explore. Keep a list of titles you like. You'll never remember them all.

I encourage you to tell or read a story each day. Some days you might offer more. Re-writing stories is a lot of fun and helps children feel that they are capable of writing their own stories. Another option is creating new stories. If they are not yet writers you or another adult will be the scribe. These stories will make a big hit if they are copied and sent home with the class. Vivian Gussin Paley, who has written a number of books on writing with preschoolers, spends time alone with the child telling the story. Later, the whole class acts out the stories of the morning. For example, one child's story was simply one word: "Mother". The group understood this and acted it out in many ways.

When re-writing stories, one method is to change the main character to another animal or person. Change the setting. Both of these differences will influence the story greatly. One example: *I Took My Frog to the Library* became *I Took My Elephant to the Suns Game.* Another way to create new stories is to set up a can full of slips with possible story settings, animals, characters or happenings that could start your new story. Encourage the children to provide new ideas to be added to the container of choices. These stories will make a big hit if they are copied and sent home with all the class members. See Chapter 17 for more about inventing stories.

Your book corner might be enhanced with Story Wheels (Chapter 13), puppets, and other stories like *Big Mac* that almost tell themselves. See Chapter 12 for Hold On Your Lap Stories. You may want to tell stories while lying on story quilts which depict simple story lines. See Chapter 11 for Quilt Stories. You might also make a book with felt pages and offer parts of a simple story to be put in order on the pages. That is a nice sequencing activity for the individual children or small groups.

Be sure to tell stories more than once so that they become familiar to the children. Include titles and authors of books or stories you use with the children in the newsletter sent home. Then parents can check favorites out of the library or purchase them for home.

Encourage parents to tell their child the story of the day they were born or adopted. Children also enjoy stories of when parents were little, grew up, got in trouble, created a mess, made a big mistake, had a good success, or enjoyed a childhood adventure. An appropriate time to introduce this idea would be when talking about families or at a family meeting with parents.

Two must-have-books to buy (or encourage your school librarian to buy) are *Mudluscious* by Jan Irving & Robin Currie and *Storyvine* by Anne Pellowski. *Storyvine* may be out of print but enough inquiries will cause the publisher to bring it back. I am on a crusade to get it back in print. Although it is out of print you will find it as a used book on Amazon.com. See the Resource Lists for more information.

If you are a storyteller...

Hello there. I bet you have some stories to share with me. I've been telling stories to groups for over thirty years. Most of my experience has been with preschool children through third grade. Many of the stories which are my favorites also, work well with school age kids. In our culture we center so early on making children grow up. I think many are still happy to be encouraged to relax and have fun using their imaginations as they did when they were younger.

I recommend two books to you from my Resources Lists. They are currently my top favorites. You may already be familiar with them. They are popular with teachers and storytellers.

Storyvine by Anne Pellowski was my first introduction to many different types of stories. She provides great examples of string stories, story wheels, drawn stories, and the idea of quilt stories. Her wisdom and experience in storytelling is inspiring. I'm hopeful the publisher will begin to publish this out-of-print treasure again. You may also find a used copy in bookstores or on the Internet.

Mudluscious by Jan Irving and Robin Currie is a book with so many original ideas that you are bound to find something there for you.

Lost, Left and All Gone is a fabulous torn-paper story that is a hit with both children and adults. *Abracadabra* is a participation rhyme for the very young. You will love both of them! These two imaginative librarians also introduced me to the idea of the story wheel which has many possibilities for young children. Their story about Mother Hubbard is their own creation but I have also used this idea with other favorite children's stories with appropriate word patterns. Some of these are:

Are You My Mother? by P.D. Eastman
Brown Bear, Brown Bear, What Do You See? by Bill Martin
Big Mac by Cindy and Eileen Hoard
The Gingerbread Boy Traditional
The House That Jack Built Traditional
Lost Left and All Gone found in *Mudluscious*
The Mitten retold by Alvin Tresselt
Old Mac Donald Had a Woodshop by Lisa Shulman
Goldilocks and the Three Bears Traditional
The Three Little Pigs Traditional
See Chapter 13 instructions about how to make a story wheel.
I know you'll add to this list.

On the list of Adult Resources you will notice some drawing books by Ed Emberly and Syd Hoff. These books have very simple drawings that most adults or children can duplicate. Since the drawings build gradually, as a story does, you can often develop a story to go with your drawing. You might like to try that. All ages love drawn stories and are often surprised by the fact that you've actually drawn something they recognize. See Chapter 8 for drawn stories.

Browse through the visuals for stories (Chapters 6-17), then choose and adapt your choices to those ideas which will make the stories you wish to tell visual. You'll find the ideas really do work to hold the attention of young children. Making the visuals I've designed will also be fun. The materials are simple, easy to find, and most are not expensive.

If you are a nanny…

If you are a nanny you are in a unique position to try out storytelling techniques. You have a captive audience and a lot of time. **You can use every idea in this book**. You are, in a sense, in every category of those who might use stories. On a daily basis you are doing most of what a parent does.

Ask yourself if you are nurturing:
- language
- manners
- toilet training
- healthy habits of eating
- hand washing
- tooth brushing
- napping
- physical activity

You are a teacher too! And storytelling will be a lot of fun.

Hopefully you and the children avoid hours of sedentary TV watching. They *can* learn things from TV but *they need interaction* with adults, other children, and materials to learn many things. They need to "Do it themselves" to really get it.

They need interaction to:
- develop expressive language
- increase vocabulary
- practice thinking
- develop problem-solving skills
- use art materials in many ways

Using art materials is important for the pleasurable process and exploration of different media. It is often a problem solving experience. Working with paper and glue is different from messing with paints. Mixing colors helps children find out how new colors are created. You can discover which colors make green, purple, orange etc. All of these experiences help children learn. Scribbling is important as a pleasurable activity, without judgment, that will end in drawing and writing in a few years. Matching picture cards sets a child up to discern those likenesses and differences necessary to tell one letter from another. The only difference between the letter *e* and the letter *c* is one short, straight line. You have to know how to see difference and likeness to read. Putting puzzles together calls for visual recognition of negative space. It takes practice to estimate which piece will fit, matching color and line. Maybe you think I'm off the subject of storytelling but I'm really trying to point out how storytelling fits into your profession and how it can make your job easier and a lot more fun.

Listening to stories being told or participating in storytelling lengthens attention. You know that the older the child, the longer the attention span. However, each child develops at his own pace and each child is to some degree the product of his experience. The child who is never read to may have little patience for listening, while another who must have a book read before bedtime will sit longer and more comfortably. When you tell stories you will notice that you and nature (natural development) are increasing the amount of time that the child can attend to something.

Retelling stories is a good activity for children. What comes first, then next…and finally how does the story end? That's story sequence and it becomes important as they begin to read. Try asking questions. What does the wolf *always* say? What does the gorilla do next? It enhances the child's expressive language when they can answer those questions. If the story has props or visual enhancement the child will often tell the story to himself or a sibling without you. Or he may pretend to read a book while turning the pages. Picture clues remind him of the story.

Vivian Gussen Paley's books offer ideas about very young children "writing" stories and acting them out. Of course, you become the notetaker for the not-yet writer. You will often have the time to use Vivian's ideas and parents are sure to treasure the results.

You know that time spent doing these very pleasurable activities is actually building abilities, practicing verbal skills, and helping the child express emotions: feelings of anger, sadness, humor, fear, happiness and satisfaction.

Re-writing favorite stories is full of possibilities. Start with a simple story and change the main character from a dog to a giraffe. Change the scene to a different place. Now, you can all begin to tell what happened. Record your new story. The children will want to read it later. See Chapter 17 for more ideas about writing stories.

Retelling well-known stories with intentional mistakes lets the child tell you what's wrong. I first read the basic idea used here in *The Read-Aloud-Handbook* by Jim Trelease. Mess up the story in any way you please. The children know how it really goes. Children love thinking they know more than you do, so they will happily tell you when you are telling it wrong. One time when I was telling a story in this way, a child asked me if I had *ever even read* the story. I've told these kinds of stories many times. You do need to be sure that the group is familiar with the original story. If they are not, they will not argue with you about how it's *really* supposed to be. See Chapter 15 for a more detailed description of how to tell a mixed-up story.

Finally, whether you are a parent, grandparent, aunt, uncle, friend, teacher, nanny or storyteller, it is clear you have an interest in delighting children. So jump in*, add to your repertoire or begin your journey as a storyteller. You are sure to have a lot of fun!*

Get going!

       Take off!

              Begin now!

                    You are ready.

What we all need, you and I, when we venture into the land
of storytelling, is to listen to another Voice, not a critic, but the
Voice of the Good Teacher we might have had, the one who adores us,
thinks we are remarkably alive, hilarious, believes in our tender,
free spirited, whoopee imaginativeness. Who says, "You are
talented, terrific, gifted, original! Go to it!"

- Chase Collins, Tell Me a Story

Try this tack. Take the pressure off yourself.
This isn't Hamlet you're working on, it's a bedtime story.
This isn't the play-offs!
You're just shooting some hoops.

- Chase Collins, Tell Me A Story

When one teaches, two learn.

- Robert Half

Chapter 3
VISUALS, VISUALS, VISUALS

WHAT are visuals? Visuals attract and hold the attention of a child or a group. Consequently, this chapter offers the most crucial concepts in this book. Capitalizing on visuals became the starting place that led to the exploration, elaboration and creation of multiple styles of storytelling. If you have worked with very young children you know that having the child's attention is everything. ***It is everything!***

If they don't want to listen, they won't!
You can't make their minds center on you. They must want to listen.
So, how can you make them want to listen?

Visuals, of course!

I taught preschool for a number of years and directed preschool teachers for even longer. Over the years as I read to children, I heard many a whiny, "I can't see the pictures." Now, the beauty of storytelling is that you *can* always see the pictures in your head. But some children and adults need a little visual hint to draw them into the story.

Maybe that is about curiosity. When I taught I knew that if I carried a paper bag or small suitcase to the center of the floor and sat down, magically, I had an audience of little bodies curious to know what I had in the bag. You can announce and announce, "Circle Time!" and some children will never come unless a teacher brings them to the group. But bring out the brown paper bag or a visual and you'll have a group beside you, **listening**. It is a simple and profound delight!

Having made that grand discovery, I began to create visual enhancements. These are simply surprises on my lap or in my bag. I never called them visuals, but that is what they are. Props, maybe, but that is not quite it either. I guess *Big Mac* was the first visual (see photo section). I love *Big Mac* because you cannot do it wrong. It is always right! You can't forget it because you know what it is, how it tastes and what its colors are. You can do it by yourself even if you are just two years old. It won't break and it's not noisy.

The story *Big Mac* was born when a woman from California told me about making a felt hamburger and using the rhyme pattern from *Brown Bear, Brown Bear What Do You See?* A hamburger is something that is very familiar to children. My daughter, Cindy, and I added purple onion, orange cheese, and green pickles to the brown bun, black hamburger, red ketchup, yellow mustard and green lettuce. Then we wrapped it in a blue wrapper. Our effort was to include as many colors as possible to help children learn colors. Cindy is Dr. Cindy, an Early Childhood Psychologist who works with inner city families. She had the little story translated for her Spanish speaking families and *Big Mac* was born bilingual. The story is often told by having the pieces distributed around the group, then added in as the story progresses, creating the hamburger. No one ever says, "I can't see…" when you're holding this visual on your lap. That's where "Hold on Your Lap Stories" originated. As I created more and more visuals I simply thought of them as stories I held on my lap. I began to list them in my workshop handouts as a category just as I listed felt board, drawn or cut paper stories.

The next "on your lap" story was *The Mitten*. In the story a tiny, black cricket tries to squeeze into the mitten with all the other bigger, creatures that are there, trying to keep warm on a snowy day. The yellow felt mitten is rigged with Velcro to come apart when the cricket tries to crawl in. Imagine the surprise when a shower of fuzzy animals descends on the children as the mitten bursts! This old Russian folktale comes to life for little kids who may never even have been cold, faced a snowstorm, or worn mittens.

About the same time I was experimenting with "Hold on Your Lap Stories" Jan Irving and Robin Currie wrote a wonderful book called *Mudluscious*, full of countless creative ideas for storytelling. The concept of the "story wheel" came from there. This visual allows the audience to participate in telling the story since, as you turn the wheel, you reveal the next character or answer a question. If the drawings are simple, the children can read the picture and help tell the story. This idea lends itself to numerous other stories in addition to the *Mudluscious* version of *Mother Hubbard*.

Some successful titles done on story wheels are:
> *Brown Bear, Brown Bear What Do You See?* by Bill Martin
> *Are You My Mother?* by P.D. Eastman
> *Goldilocks and the Three Bears* Traditional
> *The Three Little Pigs* Traditional
> *This is the House that Jack Built* Traditional
> *Old McDonald Had a Wood shop* by Lisa Shulman

These are a few examples. You are sure to discover others.

For more information and directions about story wheels see, Chapter 13 Story Wheels. In the photo section you will find a picture of a story wheel.

Some of the results you can achieve when you use visuals include:
> Holding their attention.
>> (And YOU ARE ON when you have the child's attention!
> Entertaining their fancy.
> Delighting them with language.
> Lengthening attention span.
> Teaching and expanding their vision of possibilities.
> Causing them to wonder.
> Touching other cultures.
> Connecting children with their emotions.
> Encouraging (inspiring) thought, laughter and giggles!

You can do all those fabulous 'things' with simple objects. Call them visuals, props or enhancements, they help you attract and keep the attention you want.

Some good visuals include:
> A paper bag…what's in it? It changes.
> A *Big Mac. (See Chapter 12)*

Keys…pipe cleaner keys to tell *Goodnight Gorilla*. *(See Chapter 12)*
A big yellow felt mitten and yarn animals to help tell *The Mitten*. *(See Chapter 12)*
Story wheels with attached tag board wheel to turn. (*See Chapter 13*)
String stories. (*See Chapter 10*)
Drawn stories. (*See Chapter 8*)
A magic spoon to tell a version of *Stone Soup* from *A Jar of Fools*. *(See Chapter 12)*
Blocks to tell *Fly's Castle*. *(See Chapter 12)*
A basket full of all the things in *My Little Sister Ate One Hare*. *(See Chapter 12)*
Pieces for felt board stories. (*See Chapter 6*)
A baby rattlesnake (cat toy) to tell American Indian stories. (*See Chapter 15*)
A fold of colored paper for a torn paper story. (*See Chapter 7*)
A fold of colored paper and scissors for a cut paper story. (*See Chapter 7*)
A *Pizza the Size of the Sun* and all of its parts. (*See Chapter 12*)
A cape and battered hat to tell *Greedy Old Fat Man*. (*See Chapter 14*)
A shoebox which holds items from *If You Give a Mouse a Cookie*. (*See Chapter 12*)
The Sylvester puppet to tell *Sylvester and the Magic Pebble*. (*See Chapter 12*)
A ziplock bag full of tissue paper hearts, butterflies or bits of black paper or other
    appropriate shapes. Shower the children with these at the end of stories like *Four
    Valentines in a Rainstorm* by Felicia Bond or the *Very Hungry Caterpillar* by Eric Carle.
A magic trick…glasses and a heavy piece of cord to tell *Old Lady and Her Animals*.
    (See Chapter 10)
A plate of fake chocolate chip cookies to tell and act out *The Doorbell Rang*.
    (See Chapter 12)
A toy squeaker to tell *Squeaky Old Bed*. *(See Chapter 9)*
A small baby quilt and felt animals to tell *Alligator Baby*. *(See Chapter 12)*
A larger quilt with figures from *It Looked Like Spilt Milk*. *(See Chapters 6, 11, 13)*
A Nursery Rhyme Quilt to find and say the rhymes. (*See Chapter 11*)
Caps for Sale quilt… a copy of a quilt from India. (*See Chapter 11*)
A Tortilla Quilt and *A Piñata Quilt* to tell those stories. (*See Chapter 11*)
Sweet Clara and the Freedom Quilt will help tell that story. (*See Chapter 11*)
Paper plate paddles for *I Went Walking*. (*See Chapter 13*)
A small tin of buttons to demonstrate *The Lost Button*. (*See Chapter 12*)
The Storyteller Stone. (*See Chapter 17*)
An aluminum pie tin and fake food to tell *Piggy Pie*. (*See Chapter 12*)
A white stuffed polar bear and two little ones tell *The Very Bare Polar Bear*.
    (See Chapter 12)
Three small bears dressed in Halloween costumes to tell *The Three Bears Meet
    the Three Blind Mice*. *(See Chapter 12)*
White board pens to do drawn stories. *(See Chapter 8)*
Lengths of colored string for string stories. *(See Chapter 10)*
A variety of puppets to cast as characters in stories made up by the children.

You will be able to add many other ideas to this list. Present them in a bag, a suitcase or on your lap. You will invent other enticing, imaginative ways to gain attention. In following chapters you will find detailed directions and some of my patterns for making these visuals.

It took hundreds of years for grown-ups
to realize that children have the right to be children. Slowly the child won
respect for himself and his games, interests and tastes.
- Kornei Chukovsky, Celebrated Russian Poet

Writer, Jane Yolen believes
"The eye and ear are different listeners."

Chapter 4
CHOOSING A STORY TO TELL

- Choose a story which appeals to YOU
- Select conditions familiar to the child – what can they understand?
- Match length of story to developmental level
- Consider attention span
- Look for stories that are unusual or have a surprise element
- Include stories of life experience
- Share the beauty of language

Terrific! You want to try storytelling. But which stories will you tell? You may already have some stories in mind. As you develop your own style you will be able to write your own considerations. Meantime, here are mine.

Choose a story which appeals to YOU

A story that you like is much easier to learn and tell. You will naturally give it a *warm* telling. You'll more easily find a way to make it visual (there's that word again!). You become personally attached to it more quickly. One of the first stories I told to an audience was Shel Silverstein's *Giraffe and a Half*. To this day (twenty years later) I love to start a storytelling performance by telling it because I feel so at home with it. It builds my confidence and reinforces the concept that I *am* a storyteller. It takes about ten minutes to tell. I have learned it just as Shel Silverstein wrote it, *every* word, and even adults are impressed and delighted by it. It is a funny story and I adore funny stories. It is a funny story that *even* threes and fours can understand, so it works with a lot of audiences. Choosing a story you like is the first step to successful storytelling.

Select conditions familiar to the child – what can they understand?

Is it within their experience or their fantasy? Young children lack experience and while they are much more knowledgeable than we were at their age, actual experience helps them to understand the story. When I taught four-year-olds, the astronauts had just orbited the earth; adults and children talked about space constantly. Since dramatic play usually happened when we added props to one of our centers, my partner and I made a cardboard spaceship for the children. Usually they responded quickly to "new stuff" in their play spaces, but our wonderful spaceship just sat there! Nobody played in it. Nothing happened!

We tried inviting them to play there asking, "Who wants to be the next astronaut?" We tried to stir their interest in our spaceship. Nothing worked.

As we reviewed at the end of the week we came to the conclusion that they didn't know *what to do*. What *did* astronauts do in space? As teachers we realized that we didn't know much either. *We* lacked experience. Lack of experience limited the dramatic play and it can affect your story too. The idea of man in space was so new that few people could have guessed what to do. Think about whether you should "set up" a story that you suspect is beyond the group's experience. If you even suspect some set-up would be helpful, do so with a bit of information or conversation.

Perhaps a story you like fits in the children's fantasy world! They know animals don't speak English, Spanish, or French. But, what if they *did*? What would they say? Stories of mommy or daddy animals and their babies talking make sense to all but the most literal of children. As a child you know Mom and Dad know more than you do but *what if* you *could* outsmart them or solve a mystery or a problem before they did? That is a child's dream.

Wouldn't you love to know other dreams children have? We do know they seem very real to them. Consequently, stories like *Where the Wild Things Are* have much appeal. Of course, young children have all had scary dreams. We've had scary dreams. But in this story, Max (the main character) *tames* the blue and orange monsters and makes them be quiet so that he can sleep. When he wakes up, Mommy has brought him his dinner. Earlier troubles are all forgotten. He is loved once again. That didn't really happen but, what if...? That is a child's dream...come true!

Others fantasies might involve a child:

> Showing more bravery than she thought she had
> Demonstrating more strength than he ever expects to have
> Receiving love in a totally accepted, unconditional way (Oh, we all have that dream!)
> Acting smarter than others think he is
> Proving to be a creative genius or an inventor
> Performing (maybe in the circus)
> Acting as a hero
> Finding out that others admire him or her
> Hearing and believing she/he is the greatest.

The story *Fly's Castle* by Bill Gorah is told with 6 blocks which pile on top of each other. It gives a child the chance to knock over a tower of blocks. Kids are always discouraged from knocking over blocks. How delicious to be able to knock them over, with permission! You will have to keep your eyes and mind open to find and to provide opportunities such as these in your storytelling.

What can your audience understand? How can you tell? If the audience is very young, the stories must be simple (related to their experience) and short. Attention span plays a big part in how well a story works. Feedback from the group will give you some cues as to whether they understood the story line. Ask questions such as:

> Who was chasing the Gingerbread Boy? Why?
> Was Goldilocks a polite little girl?
> Was the magic spoon really magic? Why or Why Not?
> How do we know the zookeeper was really tired?

You can sense which stories are really above their heads, if you think about it. It doesn't mean you can never use the story, it simply means you will need to wait a few months or a year before you do.

Your immediate clue indicating lack of understanding will be behavior. You will lose your audience very quickly if they don't understand what you are talking about. On the other hand, maybe they don't like the story. That's O.K. Different groups have different tastes.

Just as a negative child can influence them for ill, a positive, excited listener will attract others' attention and cause them to listen too. You don't want to lose your audience because you're telling a story that is over their heads. Kids won't let you get away with that. I don't want you to be discouraged about your ability as a storyteller when perhaps it's just the choice of material.

Also consider audience size. Group telling is trickier. A bunch of little bodies sitting close together on the floor can cause wiggles, joggles and giggles. Little hands explore and tiny feet shoot out. All can make trouble in the nicest group of children. Then too, what one group loves another finds uninteresting. Did I say groups were trickier? They are. But the challenge is worth it. Being familiar with a variety of stories will save you.

Match length of story to developmental level

While *a child's attention span grows every day it still has limits. The child will teach you what those limits are.* Pay attention to wiggles and crabbiness because that is a child's way of telling you that he has reached his limit. You are at his mercy here, but you can prevail if you pay attention and shorten your stories to meet him where he is. Over time, choose longer stories to extend attention span. A good teacher always learns more than she teaches and she learns from the children. Remember that mothers, fathers, grandmas, grandpas, sitters, and nannies know themselves to be teachers. With practice, you will learn how long your child or your group can attend to a story.

It also helps to know a bit about ages and stages of development. Two-year-olds are quite egocentric. They feel *they* are the center of the universe. They often concentrate on one character in a story and do not see the big picture. For that reason, they come to conclusions built on incomplete observations. They have much more receptive (incoming) language than expressive (outgoing) language. Louise Powell in *Ages and Stages* (a Child Development Associate Module) [CDA] says "By age three the child has about 300 expressive words, while their receptive language may number 500-900 words." This means we must listen to them and provide many chances for them to practice expressive language.

The CDA Emerging Literacy Module notes this on page twelve, "You can help by asking, 'What do you think will happen next?' This will help the child think ahead about characters and events and how the story might progress. . . .If you were writing this story what could happen next?" If children tell stories about pictures check to see that they are reading the pictures accurately.

If you are choosing for an audience of one or two, your job is easier. You'll quickly become aware of their favorite stories or types of stories. However, you do need to be sure to provide for their expressive language experiences just as you will with a larger group. At an appropriate time you can remedy faulty conclusions and briefly explain things that are not understood.

Consider attention span

The younger the child the shorter the attention span. No news there. But you may not realize that attention span is much longer "one-on-one" than it is sitting with a group. There are so many distractions sitting with a group. They are thinking so many potential thoughts:
'Do you see that little hair sticking out of that braid?'
'What is in that pocket that looks so lumpy?'
'Will he squeak if I touch him?'
'Can I get her attention if I tickle her?'

Little minds are *busy*! Therefore, stories for groups often have to be shorter than those you might consider reading or telling a child at home. However, attention span is also longer if you ***tell*** a good story than it would be if you read a good story. Most of the stories I tell to preschoolers are one to five minutes long. A few like *Giraffe and a Half* take as much as ten minutes to tell. The rhyming and colorful felt figures help to hold their attention.

The length of a child's attention span depends upon the age, temperament, developmental level, individual interest in the activity, distractions, intelligence, curiosity, and the ability of the adult to maintain the pace of the activity. Developmental articles offer little concrete evidence about how long children attend at different developmental ages. However, preschool and grade school teachers come to know the limits of their groups through observation and experience. Because of my experience, I offer some observations about the attention span of preschoolers in groups:

- *Two-Year-Olds* - may hold for 5 to 10 minutes. Some very young twos may not settle and may need to wander.
- *Three-Year-Olds* - may attend for 8 to 15 minutes. After a few weeks of school most will sit, but initially some will wander before they are able to sit. *It is a process.*
- *Four-Year-Olds* - will attend for 12 to 20 minutes.
- *Five-Year-Olds* - begin to attend as the social situation requires but may only sit comfortably for 20 minutes.

What you will notice is that every age will be able to attend longer with storytelling than with listening to stories being read. What catches and holds their attention is the direct interaction with the storyteller. It makes them feel you are doing something just for them, My advice is to err on the short side of these time limits. If you stop 'too soon' they can always beg for more!

Look for stories that are unusual or have a surprise element

I like stories that have a twist, don't you? *Alligator Baby* by Robert Munsch is a perfect example of this. In this story, Mother is having a baby. However, instead of going to the hospital Mom and Dad get lost and end up at the zoo. Then they manage to bring home a "zoo baby " instead of a "people baby." Karen, the big sister, understands the problem *and* saves the day. Kids just love stories in which they are smarter than the adults are!

Another story which anyone with a sense of humor will love is *My Little Sister Ate One Hare* by Bill Grossman. This rhymes and is a great one to memorize. "My little sister ate one hare. We thought she'd throw up then and there but, she didn't." She goes on to eat a number of other things and doesn't throw up until she eats something that is good for her. It's outrageous and funny. Most of these stories are not familiar to the children, so the surprise is new. Of course, later, when the surprises are familiar, the stories remain favorites because they are just fun! These are also good stories to rewrite because the premise can change just slightly and result in a completely different story. Both children and storytellers can rewrite stories. In the case of the non-reader, the adult becomes a note taker while the ideas come from the children. '*I Took My Frog to the Library*' became '*I Took My Elephant to a Suns Game*' in one four and five-year-old class, much to their delight.

Include stories of life experience

Every child loves hearing the story of the day they were born, including funny things like Daddy forgetting the car keys or forgetting Mother! One of my daughters arrived home, as a hungry 8-pounder, with no bottles available. Daddy thought Grandma had fixed them and Grandma thought

Daddy had done it. Also, we have a picture of our daughter, Robin, about three, pounding on the locked screen door. She was filthy, having fallen backwards into a very wet pile of mud. But I had to get some of the dirt off of her before I brought her in the house. She loves that picture and the story that goes with it. Grandma and Grandpa have lots of memories of when life was different. Being attacked on 9-11-2001 resulted in my grandchildren, Maxine and Madeline (age 15) and Cassidy (age 11) asking about Pearl Harbor. I told them about food and gas coupons, rationing, and the difficulty of getting silk stockings. Of course they asked, "What are those?" This opened the way for even more conversation. These stories offer valuable pieces of family history.

Children probably remember things you've forgotten about their own lives. Also important to them are stories of things they did as babies and as they grew up. Our family is getting out old pictures and filling granddaughter Andrea's new husband in on what she was like as a little girl. As recently as September 11, 2001 we were all eagerly telling *our* story of that day, where *we* were, how we heard about the twin towers and what we felt. We wanted to share our experience with others.

When age 12 Cassidy asked if I still had a flag quilt I had made when he was six. He lives hundreds of miles from us and had not seen the quilt for five years. But yes, I told him, I still had it. He wanted to know if I remembered that he'd told me a story about it when he was six. Of course I did. I reminded him, "We sat right there on that stairway over there while you told the story and I wrote it down." I had named the quilt "The Night the Stars Ran Away" because some of the stars had escaped the blue field and were scattered over the red and white stripes. I showed him the quilt and the story. He was delighted! Now, at thirteen, he's writing stories which he intends to turn into film scripts. The last time we visited, I told him I was going to be surprised if he did not turn out to be a writer or a director. He thanked me and then said he thought that sounded about right!

Share the beauty of language

This is evidenced in many ways. **Repetition** (including repeated lines like "I'll huff and I'll puff...") help the child become part of the story quickly because she anticipates what is to follow. It is also an asset to you, the storyteller, since it means you have fewer lines to learn. In the old Jewish tale *Something from Nothing,* each time Jacob approaches his Grandfather with a new problem the ine, " Grandfather's scissors went snip, snip, snip and his needle flew in and out" is repeated. In *I Know an Old Lady Who Swallowed a Pie* by Alison Jackson the lines build on each other and repeat to the very end.

The rhythm of the words, as in Shel Silverstein's *Giraffe and a Half*, may catch your audience. If you had a giraffe and you stretched him a half you would have a giraffe and a half. If he put on a hat and inside was a rat, you would have a giraffe and half with a rat in his hat."

Other stories are "sing-songy" and move with rhythm. For example, there is also a particular rhythm in *Too Much Noise* by Ann McGovern. Here the noises of each animal or character are listed and beg to be joined by the voices of the audience.

Some stories heighten awareness of feelings and emotions. Love, anger, fear, and sadness can often be addressed by stories that take us inside a character. Children and adults alike need to learn that feelings are O.K. and it is important that we learn to control our reaction to our feelings. Perhaps a story praises friendship as in Frog and Toad's Story of *The Lost Button* by Arnold Lobel. In this tale, Frog helps Toad look for the button he lost during a long walk. After an unsuccessful hunt, a despondent Toad arrives home to find the button right inside his own front door and realizes he has put Frog through an ordeal by being crabby and insisting on finding his button in the woods. He pulls down his sewing kit, sews all of the buttons they found onto his own jacket, and gives it to Frog. Frog knows that he and Toad are friends. **Noble qualities are best demonstrated** rather than preached about. **Some stories provide a moral**. I prefer not to moralize, but let the story do its own work in the mind of the child.

In some picture books the words flow, dance and fly, almost becoming a song or a poem. They often carry you deep inside yourself or remind you of something beautiful you once saw or felt. Putting descriptive words together in unique phrases and making comparisons or analogies helps the listener draw mental pictures. Hereby beauty of language begins to prepare the mind's palate for good tastes. We know we are all shaped by our childhood experiences. While we may not have sharp memories of those happenings, we are influenced nonetheless. Therefore, as storytellers, we should desire to offer children a taste of excellent words well put together. Some examples of this are:

> *Winnie the Pooh* by A. A. Milne
> *The Important Book* by Margaret Wise Brown
> *How the Alphabet Was Made* by Rudyard Kipling
> *How the First Letter Was Written* by Rudyard Kipling
> *A Pizza the Size of the Sun* by Jack Prelutsky
> *Giraffe and a Half* by Shel Silverstein
> *Hiawatha* by Henry Wadsworth Longfellow
> *Polar Express* by Chris Van Allsburg
> *The Night Before Christmas* by Clement Moore

Please add your own favorites.

Exposing children to new words and new arrangements of words promotes creative word use. When the language is beautifully chosen, the story is uplifted. As a rule, we do not speak so eloquently in the day-to-day, but we can still appreciate and relate to a higher standard.

Choosing a story is just the first step, but it is a crucial beginning. I do not *own* a story until I have told it two or three times. When I do I'm on the spot! I must remember the story or lose my audience. I need to give it the enthusiasm and drama that it demands. I have to have my visuals ready to go. As an audience, young children are severe critics who will let you know immediately if you have lost their attention.

As the storyteller, I need to be **on**. One way this is easier for Mom, Dad, Grandma, Grandpa or a nanny than it is for the professional storyteller is that they probably only need to tell one or two stories at a time, while the professional is likely doing a thirty to forty-five minute presentation. Finally, remember to have fun with it! You are doing this to charm and entertain children. If you are enjoying yourself, it will show and your reward will be little faces laughing, surprised and engaged. Then, when you hear, "Tell it again!" you will know it was all worth it!

This is the book I was born to write.

Sarah Ban Breathnach, author of Simple Abundance

Chapter 5
LEARNING A STORY

- Getting to know the story – reading it, reading it aloud
- To memorize or not to memorize
- Practice telling stories
- Choosing your own style
- Selling your story

Getting to know the story – reading it, reading it aloud

Let's assume you have now picked a story to learn. While you will have to discover the best way for you to learn the story, I can tell you what works for me.

- Read and re-read the story *aloud*. The repetition of your own voice helps you concentrate and imbed the story in your memory. If, like me, you do not learn stories easily, you will really have to practice.
- Concentrate on your voice, the words, and the way the story is advanced. Are there repetitious lines? This is a big help in learning a story more quickly.
- Next, tell and retell the story *aloud*. This will assist you in pinpointing your areas of weakness. Copy the text of the story onto typing pages so you don't have to turn pages. You can find parts of the text you cannot remember much faster that way. Sometimes putting notes on cards or drawing out the parts of the story you have trouble remembering will help you memorize. Typing or writing out the story provides another way to help you remember the sequence of events.

As you rehearse, you will become aware of the rhythm and feel of the story. Notice the actions or lines which have to be included to make the story work. Note these accurately. Then, learn the sequence needed to bring the story to life. What happens to the characters? Become more aware of the sequence of events by writing them in order.

In *Alice in Wonderland* the Queen tells Alice, "If you don't know where you're going, you may never get there." This is important for storytellers too. Know where you are going in the story you want to tell. What is the adventure about? Always choose key lines to remember and repeat those consistently when telling the story. There is a thread that winds through every story. You must find that thread and follow it to complete a memorable finish. If you have the story firmly in your mind, memory loss or interruption will be less of a problem for you. You can easily get back on track if you know *where* your story is going.

As you practice, be sure you are speaking loudly and clearly. If you tend to drop your voice at the end of sentences you must become aware of that. Remind yourself to smile and relax so as not to look tense. Once you are into the story session and have connected with the group of children, you'll be fine!

If you are using visual props, practice with those visuals. If it's a magic spoon ask yourself, 'How will I hold it? What will I do with it?' Look in a mirror from time to time to see what the children will see. That usually confirms, or changes what you will do when you actually tell the story. I hold my own visuals except when working with small groups. Then I prefer to pass out parts of a felt board story or other pieces and ask individual children to place them on the board as each is mentioned in the story. Participation stories are special favorites.

 If you are cutting or tearing paper, decide in advance where you will put the scraps. While children love picking up any pieces you drop, that often detracts from or interrupts the story. If drawing on a white board, predetermine where you will place pens and eraser and where you will stand. The same is true if you are using felt board pieces. Placing the pieces in the same place every time you tell the story will help you to remember the order in which items are to be recited.

Because you may be nervous or distracted by the children, you should not leave much to chance. You need all the self-confidence you can muster ahead of time. Remember, this is actually a small drama you are creating, so it takes practice and planning.

To memorize or not to memorize

Experience tells me that memorizing can be *wonderful* and occasionally *disastrous*. It is wonderful because it maintains the original language and vision of the author. You and your audience often will feel exactly what the story's creator intended. However, memorizing is disastrous if you forget the words or get lost or distracted in the telling. If it is easy for you to memorize, do it. If not, you may want to limit the number of books you choose to learn word for word.

Some stories demand learning word for word. Examples are:
> *Brown Bear, Brown Bear, What Do You See?*
> *My Little Sister Ate One Hare*
> *I Know an Old Lady Who Swallowed a Pie*
> *I'm Making a Pizza the Size of the Sun*
> *The Little Old Lady Who Was Not Afraid of Anything*
> *Giraffe and a Half*

You will likely discover others you want to learn word for word and which will become your specialty. The audience is always impressed by such a display of skill.

Most stories have *some phrases* you want to incorporate into your telling. Examples of such include:
> *Greedy Old Fat Man* - Old man what makes you so fat?"
> *No Way José* - "No way José?"
> *Alligator Baby* - "Blam, blam, blam!"
> *Jack and the Beanstalk* - "Fi, fi, fo, fum…"
> *Three Little Pigs* - "I'll huff and I'll puff and I'll blow your house down."
> *Gingerbread Boy* - "I can run away from you. I can, I can."

It is important for you to time your telling of each story. Do that a couple of times. Then note the average time on a copy of the story. This is important in planning the length of your presentation. It can also be important if you are suddenly told you have just five minutes left and you must quickly choose which story to tell.

Practice telling stories

> You have considered your choice of stories.
> You have learned the stories.
> You have your visuals and have decided how you will use them.
> You have practiced and practiced . . . aloud by yourself.
> You have made sure you are speaking loudly enough, using a pleasant tone and an animated face.

Next, it will be important to practice telling the story to some individual or small group. Choose a supportive audience. Practice goes a long way towards imbedding the story in your memory.

Choosing your own style

Now is your chance to be the storyteller YOU want to be. Some storytellers will tell you never to use character voices while others advocate using voices. Another faction says to use puppets and props while the opposition says not to do so. Some wear costumes and others never dress as characters. Other storytellers encourage memorization, telling off-the-cuff stories and dramatizing stories. We storytellers are characters. We will make fools of ourselves for a good laugh. We can make audiences laugh, cry, or wish for one more story. We are often awesome and occasionally boring. Most of all, we let you see inside of us by expressing our unique perspectives of the world. We are often shy, but find we can declare ourselves through the stories of others. Be warned, we're likely to sneak in a few stories of our own when you least expect it.

My advice is to do what comes naturally to you. Did you always, secretly, want to act? Do It! Are you nuts about puppets and hats? Wear them and make them talk! If you like visual jokes, incorporate them into your style. Create your own unique style of storytelling. Be your creative best. If you'd like to see what others say about philosophy check some of the Adult Resources listed at the end of the book.

Selling your story

They are sitting in front of you with small eager faces. Look at them individually. Catch their eyes. See how unique and beautiful they all are? Notice how they are reacting to you. Be sure your face looks friendly. You might be smiling, puzzled, fearful or tickled. Think about what message you want to send. Lean slightly toward them. You are ready to begin! Be excited about the story, characters and events. A deadpan-telling will get a deadpan response.

In most situations children should sit on the floor while you sit on a low chair to be visible to all. A child may want to sit on your lap. Discourage that if presenting to a group. Feelings are sure to be hurt since they can not all have turn to sit on your lap. The child may be wiggly, talkative or interested in your jewelry or clothing. In general, it could be distracting to you and the audience.

Keep in mind who your audience is.

**They are KIDS after all and
kids can equal *unpredictability*.**

Occasionally children will offer some new twist or possibility to the story. You may decide to incorporate that into your presentation. You may never tell the story exactly the same way twice anyway. Of course, the exception would be when you are learning a story word-for-word.

If your first story should get a less-than-excited response, change the pace. Tell a story with a different pattern. If you started with a rhyming piece, switch to a less structured narrative. You might also try speaking more slowly. Ask questions to gauge whether the audience is with you. If they are wired, do a relaxed story or perhaps a movement activity. You may have to adjust to their rhythm. Do something like *Little Green Ridinghood*, wherein you tell a familiar story with lots of mistakes. Children revel in catching those errors and your rapport will be established.

As you tell your story you may suddenly realize you've neglected to include a vital line or part. At that point you can say, "Did I forget to tell you?" Then insert the needed information and your audience will think it is part of the story. The next time they will probably remind you that you didn't say "Did I forget to tell you?" You have to be on your toes when telling tales!

One more thing, don't forget to have fun with it! You are doing this to charm and entertain children. If you have fun with it, it will show and your reward will be little faces laughing, surprised and engaged.

You can do it! You are a warrior, you are a storyteller. You won't let your audience down!

You ARE a storyteller

with an unusual gift to share, and

chances are the children, excited and impressed, will say, "Tell it Again!"

Nothing great was ever achieved without enthusiasm.

-Ralph Waldo Emerson

You've got to be careful.

If you don't know where you're going,

you might not get there.

- Yogi Berra

Chapter 6
FELT BOARD STORIES

- About felt board stories
- Storage of felt board stories
- Timing
- Practice, practice, practice
- A story list
- Making felt board stories

Felt board stories have long fascinated children. These are often repetitive or cumulative. This means the stories often repeat the same lines and add to them as the story progresses. They are inexpensive to make and last for many years. Today felt colors seem to be expanding into a vivid rainbow so you can create many beautiful, attention-getting effects.

When choosing a book to make into a felt board you need to consider a few things:
> Does the story use a limited number of characters?
> Can the story be done with one background?
> Can the story be illustrated simply?
> Can the characters be represented in felt?
> Note: You can always back paper or fabric with felt so such pieces will stick to the board.

If characters change clothes or colors, simply layer the felt right on the board. Sometimes characters move around or disappear during a story. As the storyteller, you can make this happen very easily.

As you rehearse, keep the pieces stacked in the order in which they appear in the narrative. If you leave them in the correct order after using them, they will be ready for your next presentation. At a minimum, be sure the pieces are in consecutive order before you begin telling that story. The audience will have little patience with you if you are fumbling around. You will be interrupting your own story. This is also why you must rehearse with the felt pieces you will be using. You do not want to be the one who is disruptive.

Storage of felt board pieces

Large ziplock food storage bags are one effective way to store felt board pieces. You might also use large envelopes. I prefer clear bags because they reveal contents immediately. The bags should be labeled with name and author of the story.

Here is a list of what to keep in each bag:
> Story pieces including characters and backgrounds
> A paperback copy of the book from which the story originated (when possible)
> A typed copy of the story to use when learning the text (It is helpful to laminate it.)
> Any small related visuals
> A time-length noted on the label
> Sometimes I also enclose little notes or drawings I make when learning the story.

At first, it may not seem important to store your stories in bags, but as your collection grows it saves a lot of time to do so. Another time saver is to sort the bags into categories. You choose the divisions. Some categories include Valentine's Day, Easter, Halloween, Chanukah, and Christmas. Perhaps the seasons of the year will seem a better division for you. You could also make a category for funny stories, animals, fairy tales, etc. The possibilities are endless.

Story bags can be easily kept in larger plastic storage containers. When the lid is on firmly these boxes are waterproof. They will also discourage bugs and other chewing critters from eating your story pieces!

Timing

Knowing how long it takes *you* to tell each story is important. Time your *telling, not* your *reading*, of the piece. Our pace is different when telling and reading. Do that a few times as you practice. Then you will have an average time upon which to plan. In a setting where there are time limits you will want to know whether you have time to tell a particular tale. Having, for example, twenty minutes to fill, is a significant consideration in planning your choices. Timing will also let you decide how many stories you will tell in a presentation. It may help you decide whether you can use this story with a group of two year olds, for instance. It is helpful to note your time on both the storage bag and on your copy of the story. I promise you, you will be glad to have this information.

Practice, practice, practice...

Chapter 5, Learning A Story, details how important it is to be well-rehearsed. You may wish to go back and read the chapter again. You will find that having felt characters to place on the board helps to keep the story well in mind. Be sure to practice the story at the board with the figures. Know whether you want to stand or sit and on which side of the board you are most comfortable.

If the group of children is familiar with the story, you may choose to allow some of them to help you illustrate the tale. You can hand them each a figure and explain that they will come up and put the piece on the board when their character enters the story. With every story, you want to remember where you are going. Having a destination in mind is always important.

A story list

Always consider age appropriateness. Choose stories that you will enjoy telling...it makes a difference!

A House for Hermit Crab	Eric Carle
Big Fat Enormous Lie	Marjorie Sharmat
Bremen Town Musicians	The Brothers Grimm
The Carrot Seed	Ruth Krauss
Claude the Dog	Dick Gackenbach
Elmer	David Mc Kee
Five Leftover Pieces of Pizza	*Mudluscious*
Giraffe and a Half	Shel Silverstein
Henny Penny	Traditional English Fairy Tale

Ice Cream Cone Scoopers	*Mudluscious*
I Know an Old Lady Who Swallowed a Pie	Alison Jackson
Joey	Jack Kent
More Hole than Sock	*Mudluscious*
The Most Wonderful Egg in the World	Helme Heine
Nine in a Line	Ann Kirn
Oh, What a Cake	*Mudluscious*
Picky Paul	*Mudluscious*
Seven Eggs	Meredith Hooper
Simple Pictures are Best	Nancy Willard
Six Crows	Leo Leonni
The Little Old Lady Who Was Not	
Afraid of Anything	Linda Williams
The Mixed-Up Chameleon	Eric Carle
Thomas' Snowsuit	Robert Munsch
Too Much Noise	Ann McGovern
Whiffle Squeak	Carol Lee Cohen

Add your favorites and keep watching for new tales to add to this list.

Making felt board stories

You will need:

- A steam iron
- Tacky glue
- Good felt colors
- Sharp scissors
- A few toothpicks
- A permanent black marker

- If your felt is wrinkled, press it lightly with a steam iron set on medium heat.
- Do not leave the iron in one place or the felt will shrink.
- Shop for true colors as well as lovely shades of color. Use true color when you want a young child to identify that color. Older children know there are many shades of every color but beginners need to be able to see a red red or a blue blue.
- Toothpicks are helpful when gluing pieces together. Fingers get sticky and fuzzy quickly while toothpicks let you tuck, push or press down on a tiny eye or other small pieces.
- Draw the figures on paper first. Then cut out patterns. Next, pin the pattern to felt and cut the felt piece. Illustrators naturally copyright their illustrations so it is not possible to give you patterns for most things. Simple shapes with details done with permanent markers will do for many characters.
- Save your patterns. You may lose a piece and need to replace it or a friend may ask to use it to create her own copy of the story. Another reason to keep patterns is that you might lose a story and want to replace it.

I have also made my own felt board by covering my white drawing board with a removable felt cover. Then, of course, I needed a carrier for those pieces. You can see how I did all of this in Chapter 19, Bits and Pieces.

I make my felt characters and pieces with great care. When appropriate, I may add sequins, ribbons or other materials. It is worth the time to create interesting pieces that will capture the audience. Colorful, detailed pieces elevate the story and will definitely add to your presentation. This old standby is still a very effective way to make a story come alive. Having the figures in your hands also helps you remember the story and its sequence. Later, the children may choose to create their own dialogue for the characters as they re-enact your story...or make up a new one.

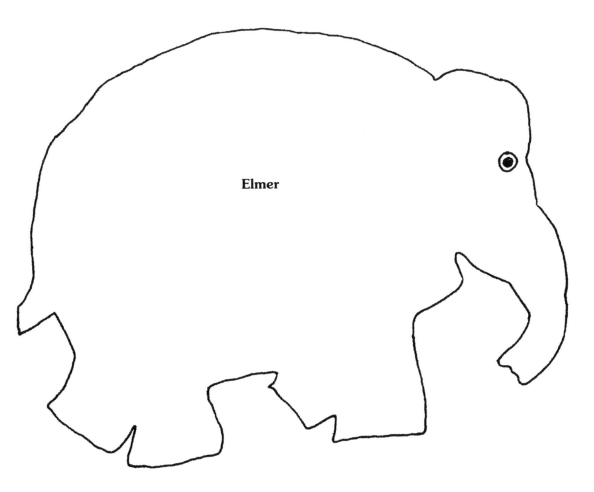

Elmer

ELMER
by David McKee

Directions:

1. Read the story first.

2. Cut two each of the seven elephants from gray felt.

3. Leave one elephant of each size gray.

4. Decorate Elmer using small bright squares of felt and Tacky glue. Add Elmer's ear. Consult book for pictures.

5. Decorate one set of the remaining six elephants for the "Elmer's Day Parade". Use felt scraps and Tacky glue to show that those elephants were very creative. You will notice that Elmer is gray in the parade.

6. Add eyes to all elephants with permanent black marker.

7. Make three imaginative plants. Use scraps and make three plants or trees that you have never ever seen.

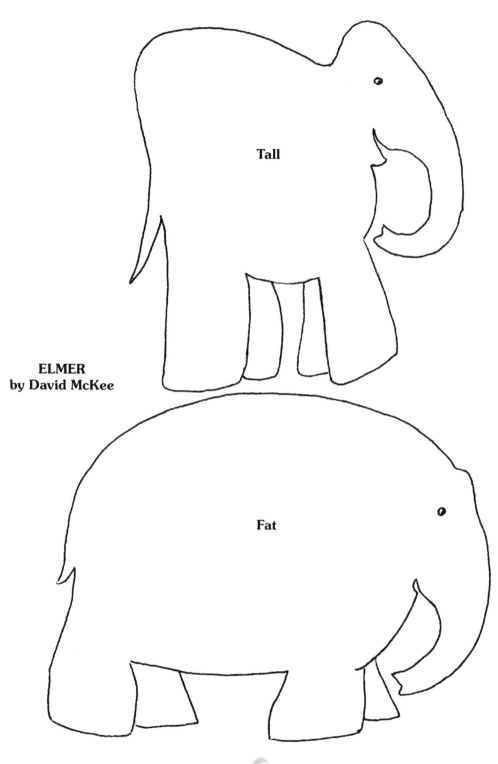

Tall

ELMER
by David McKee

Fat

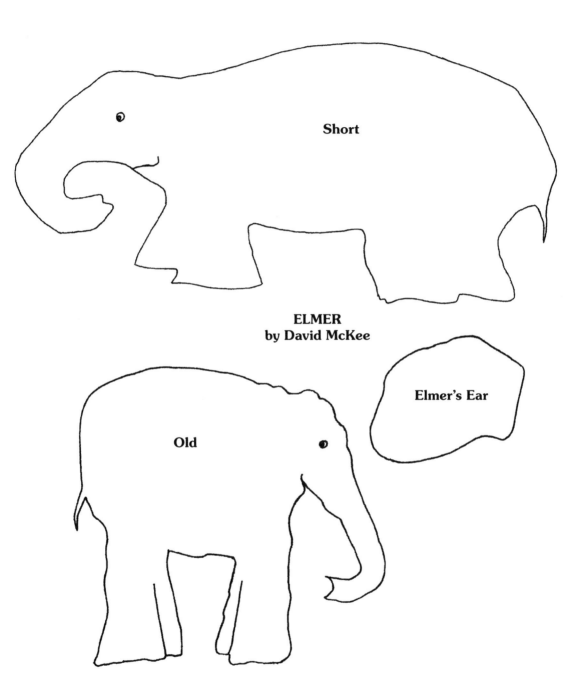

Short

ELMER
by David McKee

Old

Elmer's Ear

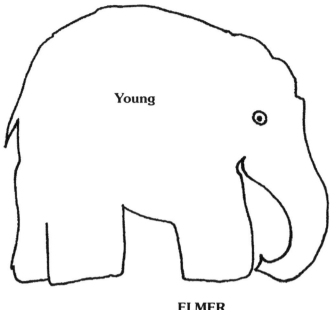

Young

ELMER
by David McKee

Skinny

Gray cloud

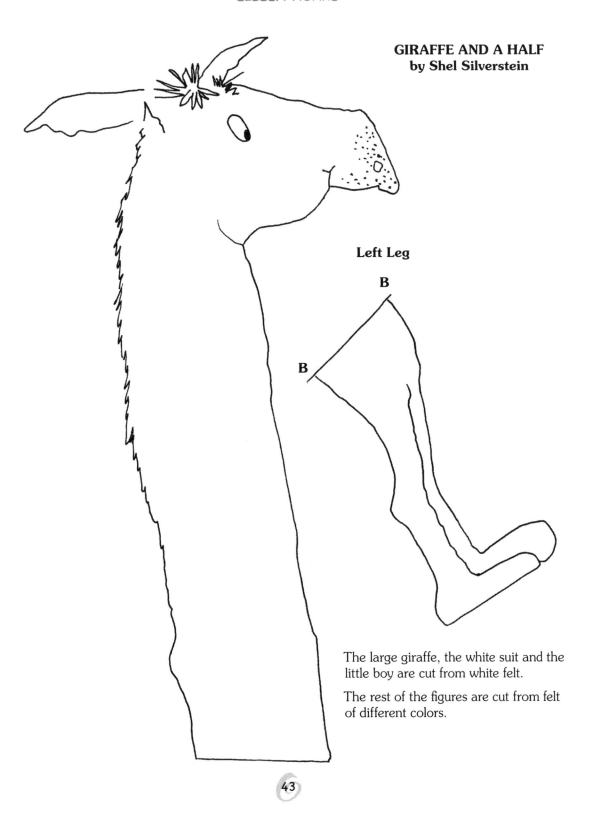

GIRAFFE AND A HALF
by Shel Silverstein

Left Leg

B

B

The large giraffe, the white suit and the little boy are cut from white felt.

The rest of the figures are cut from felt of different colors.

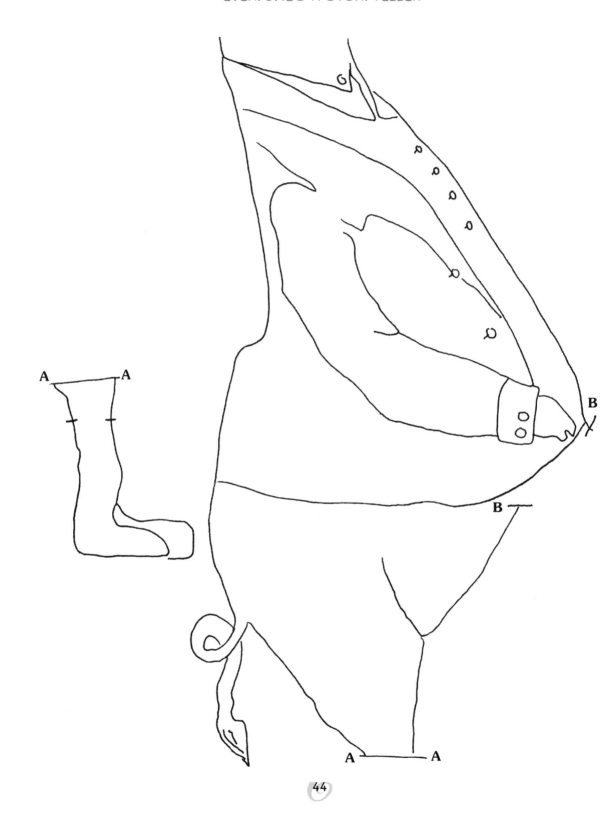

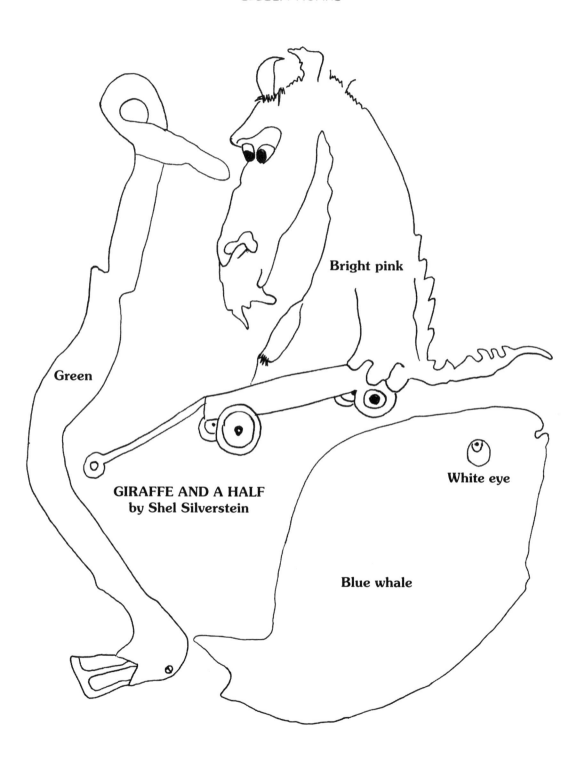

Bright pink

Green

White eye

GIRAFFE AND A HALF
by Shel Silverstein

Blue whale

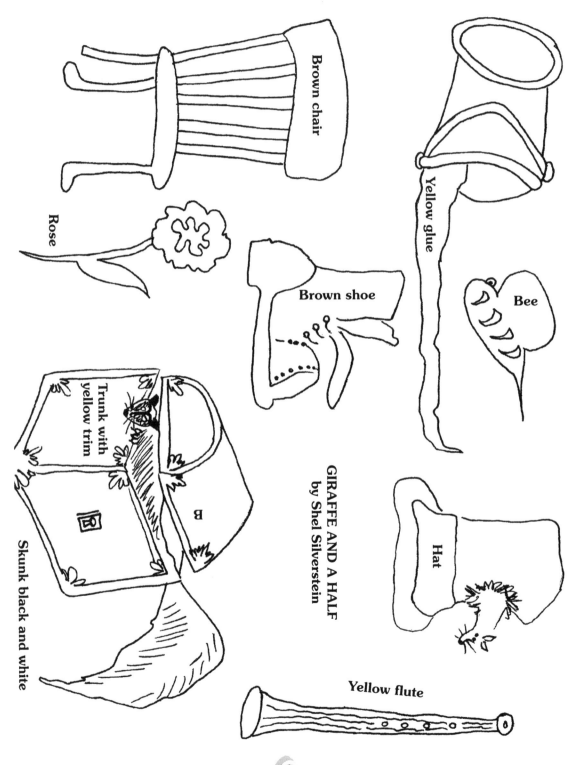

Brown chair

Yellow glue

Rose

Brown shoe

Bee

Trunk with yellow trim

B

GIRAFFE AND A HALF
by Shel Silverstein

Hat

Skunk black and white

Yellow flute

GIRAFFE AND A HALF
by Shel Silverstein

Red bike

Boy -
all white
with details
drawn with a
permanent
black
marker

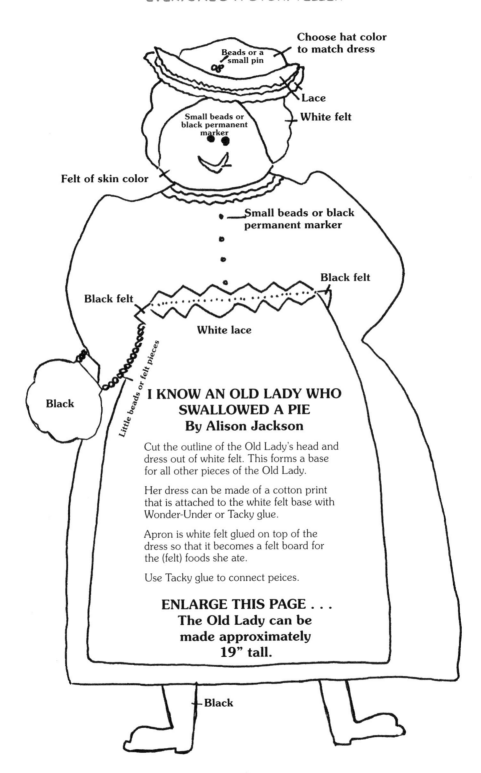

Choose hat color to match dress

Beads or a small pin

Lace

White felt

Small beads or black permanent marker

Felt of skin color

Small beads or black permanent marker

Black felt

Black felt

White lace

Little beads or felt pieces

Black

I KNOW AN OLD LADY WHO SWALLOWED A PIE
By Alison Jackson

Cut the outline of the Old Lady's head and dress out of white felt. This forms a base for all other pieces of the Old Lady.

Her dress can be made of a cotton print that is attached to the white felt base with Wonder-Under or Tacky glue.

Apron is white felt glued on top of the dress so that it becomes a felt board for the (felt) foods she ate.

Use Tacky glue to connect peices.

ENLARGE THIS PAGE . . .
The Old Lady can be made approximately 19" tall.

Black

I KNOW AN OLD LADY WHO SWALLOWED A PIE
By Alison Jackson

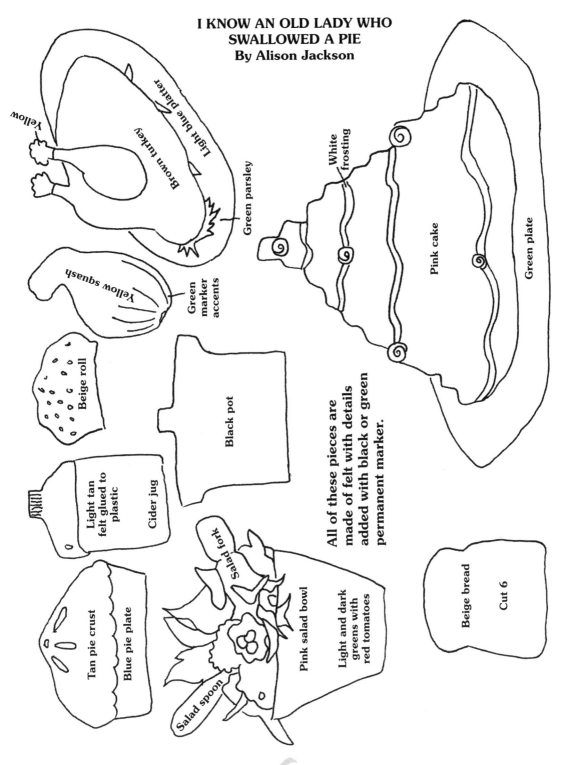

Yellow

Light blue platter

Brown turkey

Green parsley

White frosting

Pink cake

Green plate

Yellow squash

Green marker accents

Beige roll

Black pot

Light tan felt glued to plastic

Cider jug

All of these pieces are made of felt with details added with black or green permanent marker.

Salad fork

Tan pie crust

Blue pie plate

Salad spoon

Pink salad bowl

Light and dark greens with red tomatoes

Beige bread

Cut 6

TOO MUCH NOISE
By Ann McGovern

Color these drawings.
Cut out around each
animal leaving 1/4" - 1/2"
of white paper showing.

Use Tacky or spray glue
to attach to pieces of felt.

Make a copy of this page and color it.

TOO MUCH NOISE
By Ann McGovern

Leave the interior of the house in one piece and mount on felt.

Nothing great was ever
achieved without enthusiasm.

- Ralph Waldo Emerson

You've got to be careful.
If you don't know where you're going
you might not get there.

- Yogi Berra

Chapter 7
CUT, FOLD AND TEAR PAPER STORIES

* *Five Little Foxes in the Snow* by Tony Johnston
* *Little Bunny's Dream* by Eileen Hoard
    Little Orange House originally published in 1982 in Highlights Magazine
    also found in *The Family Storytelling Handbook* by Anne Pellowski and
    Paper Stories by Jean Stangl
Lost, Left and All Gone found in *Mudluscious*
Mr. Willowby's Christmas Tree by Robert Barry
* *One Elephant Went Out to Play* a Traditional singing game
Pine Tree's Great Surprise found in *Paper Stories* by Jean Stangl
Something from Nothing by Phoebe Gilman
The Red Woolen Blanket by Bob Graham
What Am I? found in *Paper Stories* by Jean Stangl
* *Who's in the barn?* found in *Paper Stories* by Jean Stangl

Stories with asterisks are cut from folded fans.
See the end of this chapter for a few patterns and how/to make fans.

In Chapter 7 you'll find examples of stories that work well with cut, folded or torn paper. This is another example of creating attention with the unknown. What *will* you do with that piece of paper? The audience is waiting to find out.

Cut, fold and tear paper stories fascinate an audience because they tickle the curiosity. You may use a variety of papers for these stories. Colored construction paper or bright copy papers are the easiest to locate. Scrap paper, envelopes, newspaper, and napkins will all work in a pinch. However, if you are telling your story to a group, the effect is usually enhanced by using paper of an appropriate color, size and weight.

Cutting or tearing paper while you tell the story is somewhat like patting your head and rubbing your tummy at the same time. That means you must master the telling and the cutting separately and then practice doing them at the same time. These are most often short stories, so timing is not as important as it is with drawing and telling. As long as your story ends soon after you finish tearing or cutting, the effect will be satisfactory.

For some cut or torn paper stories I merely identify a significant figure or shape related to the story. As I tell the story I cut out paper that has been folded like a fan so that a string of images result. Once the paper is folded correctly, I lightly draw the figure I wish to cut out on the top fold of my 'fan'. No one ever seems to notice this and you are likely to feel more secure as you cut the shape.

You can also do simple origami as you tell a story. However, since you must fold the paper on a flat surface, this may work better with just a few children than it will with a group. If the audience cannot see what you're doing you risk losing their attention.

Later in this chapter you will find specific directions for folding and cutting paper to create strings of mittens, reindeer or whatever. It is easy to do, but if you don't make the correct folds and cuts you will not have a string of shapes. You will have separate shapes that are not connected. There are also patterns for cutting the figures for *Something from Nothing, Five Little Foxes in the Snow, One Elephant Went Out to Play* and *Little Bunny's Dream*. Be sure to explore *Mudluscious*, especially for the great story, *Lost, Left and All Gone*.

The following are brief descriptions of the stories listed above.

Five Little Foxes in the Snow by Tony Johnston is about little foxes playing in the snow while Grandma sits by the fire knitting mittens as a surprise. An easy image here is a string of red mittens. By the time you have finished cutting the mittens, the story has come to an end and the little foxes have a whole string of new red mittens. A pattern is found later in this chapter.

One day I tried my hand at creating a cut paper story. The result follows:

Little Bunny's Dream

by Eileen Hoard

One night Little Bunny had a dream. He dreamed of a beautiful egg. It was painted with every color of the rainbow. His dream seemed quite real. When he woke up he asked his mom if she would please get him a bunny egg. He called it a "bunny egg" because he saw it in his "bunny dream".

His mom just laughed and told him, "There's no such thing as a bunny egg." So he started out to find one for himself. Soon he saw a hen.

"Do you know where I can get a bunny egg?" he asked the mama chicken.

"There's no such thing as a bunny egg," clucked the indignant hen.

He kept looking for a bunny egg just like the one he had seen in his dream. He walked along and walked along until he met a robin digging for worms. He asked her if she knew anything about bunny eggs.

"There's no such thing as a bunny egg," cheeped the busy mama robin.

Still, he wasn't discouraged. Maybe a mother hummingbird would know where he could get the egg he wanted. Finally he saw one of the small birds. He called to her, "Oh, oh, mama hummingbird, do you have a bunny egg?" "There's no such thing as a bunny egg," hummed the little bird. She flew by in such a big hurry she didn't even stop. All he actually heard was, "...no such thing."

He even asked an airplane about a bunny egg. But he got no answer. Maybe tonight he would dream of a whole row of bunny eggs. Slowly he hopped home. All the while he was thinking. When he got home he got out some paper, a pair of scissors and brightly colored markers.

> [The storyteller takes out a piece of paper. The paper is folded in half with a colorful bunny egg already drawn on the inside. The storyteller cuts out one half of an egg shape, then opens the paper to reveal the colorful bunny egg.]

There was the egg just as he remembered it! His wonderful egg was inside. It was made with all the beautiful rainbow colors he had dreamed about. He showed it to his mom. "What a good dream, you had," said his mom. "I guess there is such a thing as a bunny egg after all. But you're tired. Go to bed and see if you can dream of a different bunny egg tonight." And he did!

The next day his mom said, "You know, I'm still not quite sure there is such a thing as a bunny egg. I think real bunny eggs are only in your dreams." But Little Bunny knew better!

The next night he dreamed of a whole ROW of bunny eggs.

[Here the storyteller can cut out a whole row of colorful bunny eggs.]

You might ask your child or group of children, "Do you think the things you see in *your dreams* are real?" You may be surprised by their answers. It may provide subjects for further conversation. Be sure to share *your answers* to such questions with them also.

Little Orange House is a Halloween story. You need one 9"x12" piece of orange paper and a pair of scissors. As you tell this story, you will end up cutting out a Jack-O-Lantern that, as it turns out, is also a witch's house. It is quite fun!

Lost, Left and All Gone is always a surprise to the audience. You need one 9"x12" piece of brown paper folded in half and cut into the shape of a loaf of bread. It is also necessary to draw a small eye on the inside of the folded paper. Do this in advance.

As a young boy named Mojo walked through the jungle on his way home from a shopping trip to the village, he dropped one of his loaves of bread. Soon the wild animals came to nibble on it. When Mojo came back through the jungle looking for his bread he did not find it, but he did find a surprise. When you read the story in *Mudluscious* you will know why you need to draw an eye on the inside of the folded brown paper. You will find a pattern for this story later in this chapter.

My favorite story to do in cut paper is **Mr. Willowby's Christmas Tree**. Published as a Weekly Reader Children's Book Club edition, this is a charming little Christmas story from 1963. It is evidently a memorable story because a woman once called me to ask about it a year after I had presented it. She told me most of the story. But she could not remember the title and wondered if I could tell her how to find it. I loaned her my copy of the book.

A short version of the story is that Mr. Willowby has a tree that is too tall for his spacious living room, so he cuts off the treetop and throws it out. Animal after animal picks up the little leftover tree. It is reduced in size each time, as each new owner needs a smaller tree.

[You will start out with a rather large tree that you have cut out of green paper. I often use bulletin board paper that is 48" wide and can be cut as long as desired. As you tell the story, **tear or cut off** the treetop. Continue to **hold the treetop as you tell the rest of the story**. This is the part the animals use for their Christmas trees. You will tear off smaller parts of the treetop, discarding the bottom piece of the tree. Cut out your own Christmas tree relative to the size of paper available to you.]

One Elephant Went Out to Play is a singing game played by young children as they move around the room or playground swinging both arms as a trunk. You will find the words and a pattern for a string of cut paper elephants later in this chapter.

Pine Tree's Great Surprise is found in *Paper Stories* by Jean Stangl. She has a pattern for it in her book. It is a simple story of Pine Tree who no longer looks like a Christmas tree because his top has broken off in a lightning storm. He is very sad. His friends in the forest decide to do something to cheer him up. All of the animals help by doing what they do best. What they do really pleases Pine Tree. Read it to find out!

Something from Nothing by Phoebe Gilman is a longer story. This is actually an old Jewish tale, retold. When Joseph is a baby his grandfather makes a blue blanket for him. As time passes, the blanket becomes tattered and spotted. Mother wants him to throw it out. But Joseph repeatedly takes it to Grandpa who manages to make it into something else. So, the teller keeps cutting the blanket down. First he tailors a jacket for Joseph. Then he cuts the jacket down to a vest. The vest becomes a handkerchief. The handkerchief turns into a tie and finally the tie is made into a button. *In the end the button is lost and Joseph has nothing, except, just enough…to make a good story.* The pattern is found later in this chapter.

The Red Woolen Blanket is the easiest torn paper story to do. On one side of a sheet of red paper you can print your short version of the story. This makes it very easy to review the story before you tell it. No one seems to notice that the paper has printing on it.

> [As you tell the story you only need to tear pieces off of a red 9"x11" sheet of paper. You must be sure to end up with a piece the size of a postage stamp. Since tearing this story is so simple you will find it relatively stress free.]

Here's why! The red, wool, baby blanket meets with a few accidents along the way and it keeps getting smaller and smaller as the little girl grows up. Soon the baby is a little girl who is off to her first day of school. That postage stamp-sized scrap is all that is left of the well-loved, red, wool, baby blanket. She takes it to school with her. The events of the day prove interesting and satisfying. If you know a child who has a special blanket, he/she will certainly enjoy this story.

What Am I? is found in *Paper Stories* by Jean Stangl. It is a little easy riddle. Cut out the answer as you recite the rhyming lines. Everyone can do this cut paper figure.

In **Who's In the Barn?** by Jean Stangl, a jolly old man in a red suit pulls his sled to his barn. Who was that old man and who is in the barn? As the story draws to a close, a string of brown reindeer is unfurled. The last one has a red nose. (The children all know his name is Rudolph!) If you can fold paper and cut, you can do this stuff! The delight is the surprise you create. Of course, if the group is small you can always give each child a memento of the tale you've cut!

Young children love any excuse to stand up or leave the group. When you are cutting or tearing paper, scrap pieces may drop to the floor. Children will scramble to pick them up. A flat box or small basket held on your lap will catch your scraps and avoid a disturbance. I learned this hint *the hard way.*

It will be quite easy for you to make a number of existing stories visible when you add cut or torn shapes to the story. You may also find you can write a simple story and cut a shape to represent it. In addition, you can fold shapes like a pig and a dog. You will find directions for these later in this chapter. They are easy to make and you may choose to put both into the same story. For more folded shapes, consult a book of simple origami.

Experiment with cutting and folding paper. You will create new and different effects. Keep the shapes you cut simple as you are often cutting through many layers of paper. Encourage the children in your life to experiment with this too. Spend some time with the book *Paper Stories* by Jean Stangl. It will motivate you to continue this form of storytelling.

Creativity can be described as letting go of certainties.

- Gail Sheehy, Writer

Children think in terms of images.

- Kornei Chukovsky, Celebrated Russian author From Two to Five

A singer cannot delight you with his singing unless
he himself delights to sing.

- Kahlil Gibran

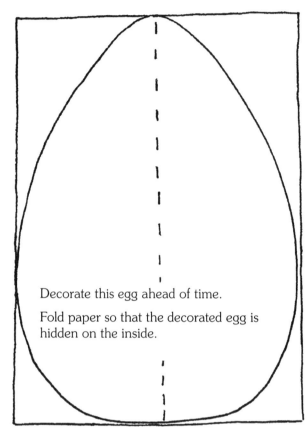

Decorate this egg ahead of time.

Fold paper so that the decorated egg is hidden on the inside.

Little Bunny's Dream

This big egg starts with paper 3-3/4" x 5-1/4". Fold in half vertically. Scribble or draw a large design on the inside of the rectangle. Your audience will not see it. Fold the paper in half and hold it that way as you cut and tell the story.

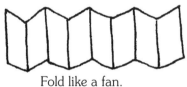

Fold like a fan.
Crease the folds well.

Of course, you must prefold the fans. It won't hurt to fold more than you think you will need. That way you are prepared for the request to "do it again."

2" x 1-1/2"

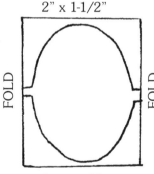

A piece 9" long will let you cut 6 eggs.

You can lightly draw the pattern on the top fold of the fan. Check to see that you are cutting the figure so it is connected to the next figure.

Draw a design on each panel before you plan to tell this story. Designs can be a quick scribble, the excess will be cut off.

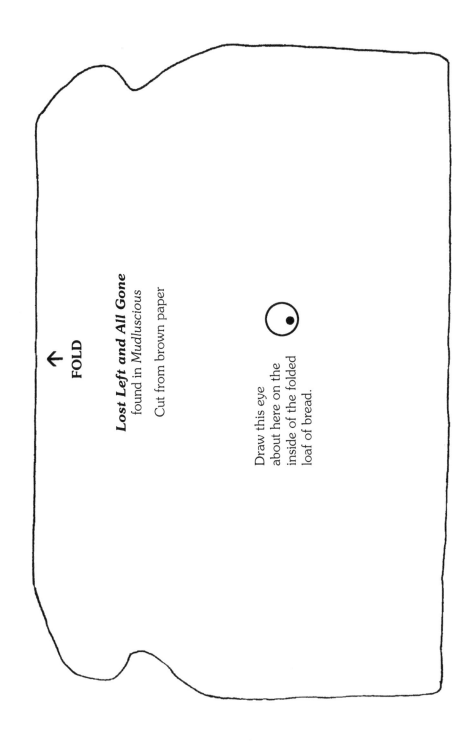

FOLD

Lost Left and All Gone
found in *Mudluscious*

Cut from brown paper

Draw this eye about here on the inside of the folded loaf of bread.

One Elephant Went Out to Play

A traditional children's singing game

One elephant went out to play
in a spider's web one day.
He/she had such enormous fun
he/she called for another
elephant to come.

Two elephants went out to play
in a spider's web one day.
They had such enormous fun
they called for another
elephant to come.....

Continue adding a new number as you
begin each new verse.

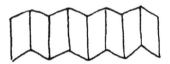

Fold like a fan.
Crease the folds as well.

3-3/4" x 2-1/2"

18" will afford 5 elephants.

Of course, you must pre-fold the fans. It
won't hurt to fold more than you think
you will need. That way you are prepared
for the requests to "Do it again."

You can lightly draw the pattern on the
top fold of the fan. Check to see that you
are cutting the figure so it is connected to
the next figure.

Your audience will not realize you are cutting on pre-drawn lines.

Five Little Foxes in the Snow
by Tony Johnston

1-3/16" x 2"

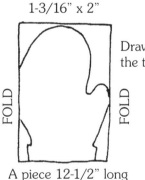

Draw pattern onto
the top fold of the fan.

A piece 12-1/2" long
will afford 10 mittens.

Fold a strip of paper into a fan.
Crease the folds well. Draw a
mitten on the top fold. Make
certain when you cut that the
mittens will be connected.

Gather the fan into a flat fold
so that you can cut through all
of the folds at the same time.

Pig and Dog

These are easy figures to fold.
Use them alone or with a story.
Both start with a square folded
into a triangle. Then, corners
are folded to create ears.

FOLD

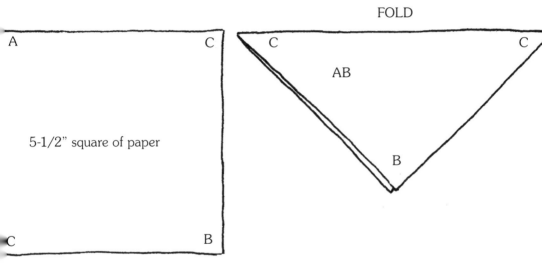

Fold both corners 'C' to create ears.
Add eyes and nostrils.

Fold both corners 'C' to create ears.
Add eyes, a small nose and dots for whiskers.

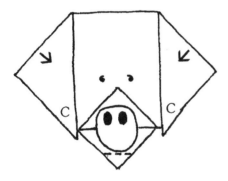

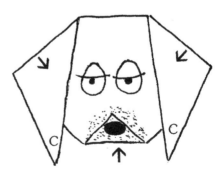

Fold only the top 'C' up
for a large nose. Fold tip
of chin under.

Fold both 'B's' up for
a small nose. If desired
you can glue both
'B's' down.

I have changed the story
so that you are cutting
figures in this order:

1. Blanket   4. Handkerchief
2. Jacket   5. Tie
3. Vest   6. Button

Something from Nothing
by Phoebe Gilman
A cut paper story

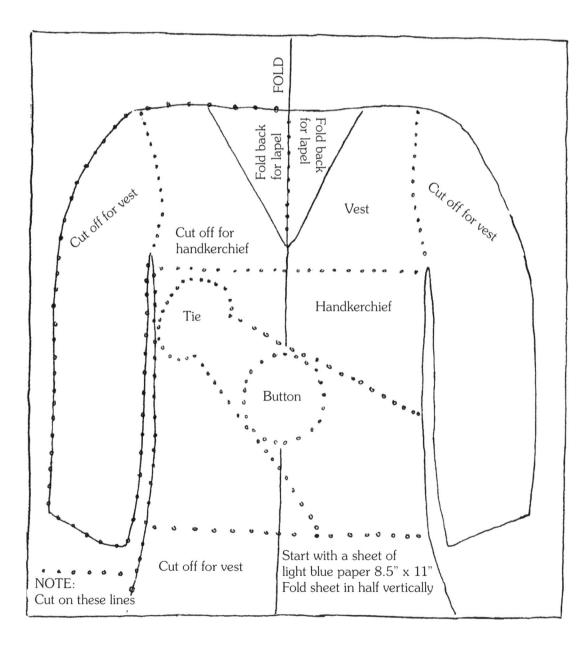

FOLD

Fold back for lapel

Fold back for lapel

Cut off for vest

Vest

Cut off for vest

Cut off for handkerchief

Handkerchief

Tie

Button

Cut off for vest

NOTE:
Cut on these lines

Start with a sheet of
light blue paper 8.5" x 11"
Fold sheet in half vertically

After listening to
Wild Bird, Mason,
who had just turned five,
drew her own version
of the story.

Chukovsky was a champion of the child's right to grow according to his inherent child's nature, to savor all kinds of experiences and literary fare and to benefit from the value of nonsense verse and fairy tales.

Taken from the preface of the book From Two to Five

Written by Miriam Morton

Chapter 8
DRAWN STORIES

Stories by others:
The Black Cat as told in *Storyvine*
The Ghost on Pedersen's Farm by Richard Thompson from *Frog's Riddle*
Dinosaur source unknown
Wild Bird told in the *Storyvine*
Witches House the original source: Highlights Magazine and also found
    in the *Family Storytelling Handbook* by Anne Pellowski

Stories by Eileen:
Crash, Crash, Crash by Eileen Hoard
Cuddles by Eileen Hoard
Drawing Halloween Pictures by Eileen Hoard
Jamie's Surprise by Eileen Hoard
Mojo's Walk by Eileen Hoard
Natalie's Story by Natalie and Eileen Hoard
Talking to Grandpa by Eileen Hoard
Thanksgiving Day Dinner by Eileen Hoard
The Scribbled Dog by Eileen Hoard
The Very Busy Spider by Eric Carle with a drawing by Eileen Hoard
This is My Picture by Eileen Hoard

These books lend themselves to being drawn by YOU, the creative storyteller:
Drawing Lessons from a Bear by David McPhail
A Present for Mother by Frank Asch
Bread and Honey by Frank Asch
Draw Me a Star by Eric Carle
Harold and the Purple Crayon by Crockett Johnson
The Birthday Present adapted by Valerie Garfield
Sandcake by Frank Asch

Drawing is a great attention-getter. All ages are attracted to someone who is drawing. Most people are convinced that artists have a very special talent which they do. But many of us think *we* cannot draw because someone has told us we did not draw very well. Or, worse, we have been laughed at for drawing anything at all. Don't allow that to stop you as you will miss a lot of fun. The good news is that we draw every time we write. So, we can all duplicate a drawing done with curves, circles and straight lines.

I remember my grandmother drawing a rambling story for my sister and me. As the story ended we saw a cat. I have never found that story anywhere in print. Of course, my memory of it is rather fuzzy. I know that there may have been as many versions of it as there were people who told it.

The version titled *The Black Cat* in *Storyvine* is very similar to my Nana's story. I think you'll enjoy it.

If you keep your drawings simple you will be able to talk and draw at the same time. I usually draw on a large white board with colored, dry erase, white board pens. Of course, your drawings can be done with crayon, pen, pencil or marker on paper of any size. In a pinch you may even use a napkin or an envelope. Anything will do, as long as your audience can see the pictures. If you're using a white board, be sure to provide a white board eraser or a piece of paper towel to get rid of mistakes and to clear your board for the next story.

When I first saw the drawing of *Wild Bird* and its story in *Storyvine*, I was delighted with it. I began to tell it and others like it. Soon I took some baby steps and created *The Thanksgiving Day Dinner* and *Drawing Halloween Pictures.* Then I found the very simple drawing books, created for children by Syd Hoff and Ed Emberley (see Adult Resources for specific titles). I was able to connect some characters I imagined to some of their drawings. Later, I ventured into some drawings of my own like *Crash, Crash, Crash, Jamie's Surprise* and *This is My Picture.* I also collaborated with ten-year old Natalie, who told me the beginning of a story that I now call *Natalie's Story.*

You will find other unique, drawn stories in *Frog's Riddle* and *Draw-and-Tell,* both by Richard Thompson. My favorite is *The Ghost on Pedersen's Farm* found in *Frog's Riddle.* Here, you trick your audience through most of the story. They simply cannot figure out what you are drawing. At the end, turn the drawing upside down to reveal *a cow,* instead of *the ghost* they *thought* you were trying to draw.

Such drawings are guaranteed to entertain. Depending on the age, some children can quickly learn to draw and tell these stories for their own small audience of adults or kids. Inventive children may decide to create stories of their own. Encourage them to do that! Who knows? You may decide to create some stories yourself. Just do it!

Another way to discover stories is to watch for drawings that have a story to tell. Choose drawings with limited detail and obvious meaning. Doodle, scribble and cartoon your ideas. Warm up with *Droodles* by Roger Price. This is a book of simple drawings with multiple meanings. You might even try doodling with your non-dominant hand to encourage the child in you to express itself.

When you develop a story and drawing, write the words of the story beside the part of the drawing they accompany. *Change pen color as appropriate.* For example, in my story *Drawing Halloween Pictures* I use green for the stem, orange for the lines of the pumpkin, and black for much of the rest.

dd another dimension to a drawn story using colored paper. Cut out a shape and mount it on a
heet of another color. You can draw on this two-layered paper by attaching it to an easel or your
hite board. In Ed Emberley's *Drawing Book of Faces* he creates his faces on a colored shape.
ince this is mounted on another piece of paper, you now have a background so you can easily
dd hair, hats, earrings, ties etc. All kinds of drawings can be created from basic shapes: ovals,
rcles, squares, rectangles and triangles. Once you try it you will see how this simple device adds
nother dimension to your drawings. My example shows you how an unusual shape might be
urned into a giant, another person or animal with just a few quick lines.

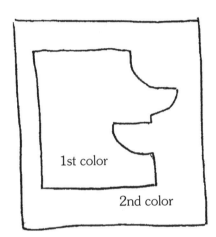

1st color

2nd color

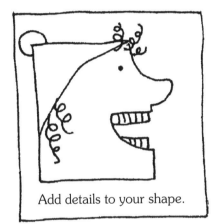

Add details to your shape.

The Scribbled Dog

by Eileen Hoard

Another technique used by Ed Emberley is the use of scribble drawings. I made up this little riddle
game to go with the idea of his scribbled dog.

This is my special dog who tells stories.
 asked him, "What story do you have today?"
He said he was taking a walk and as he did
he stopped to smell things.

The first thing was green and looked like
a really long snake.
Do you know what it was?" he asked.
   A garden hose!

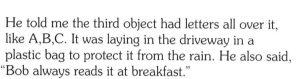

The second item was black, white,
and round. I've seen kids kicking it around.
The dog asked, "Can you guess what it was?"
   A soccer ball!

He told me the third object had letters all over it,
like A,B,C. It was laying in the driveway in a
plastic bag to protect it from the rain. He also said,
"Bob always reads it at breakfast."
What do you think it was?
   A newspaper!

Then he said, " I hear Bob calling me. He's my
friend who feeds me, brushes my fur
and likes for me to sit by him so he can pet
me. I let him think he owns me. But
actually I own him!"

This could be an ongoing story. The
riddles may change over time.
It is a good thinking game.

The next is along the same line.

Cuddles

by Eileen Hoard

Cuddles, the cat, plays Clues. Using clues she wants you to guess what she wants or what she's thinking about. For example, these are the clues she gave me one at a time the other day. She said, "It's soft with hard things inside. It can be blue, red, green, yellow, gray, or white. Most often it is brown. It lives in trees and it flies."

Finally I guessed it was a bird! It was!
This is a good game even if you don't draw it since it causes children to think and sort out ideas. Finally, if they give you clues, it provides experience using expressive language.

Here is one last idea.

I own a small book titled *Rock Art Symbols of the Southwest* by Rick Harris. Soon, I plan to incorporate a number of these symbols into a story. To draw this story I will only have to produce symbols for the nouns or major words, adding all adjectives, articles and adverbs orally. The bonus value lies in alerting children to symbols and to how people have tried to communicate their stories before they had use of the written word. We are all storytellers. We all have a story to tell. Try to stop us!

Keep drawing! The subjects and ideas are endless!

Dinosaur

Source Unknown

One day a little girl was
walking along. Wherever she
put her foot, she left a footprint.

As she walked along, she went
up and down the mountains.

Then she came to a long lake which
had some hills at one end.

She walked along and walked along
and soon she came to four houses.

Way off in the distance she saw a dot.
She hurried toward it and as she got
closer she saw . . .
THAT IT WAS A DINOSAUR!

*(or you may make the character a boy)

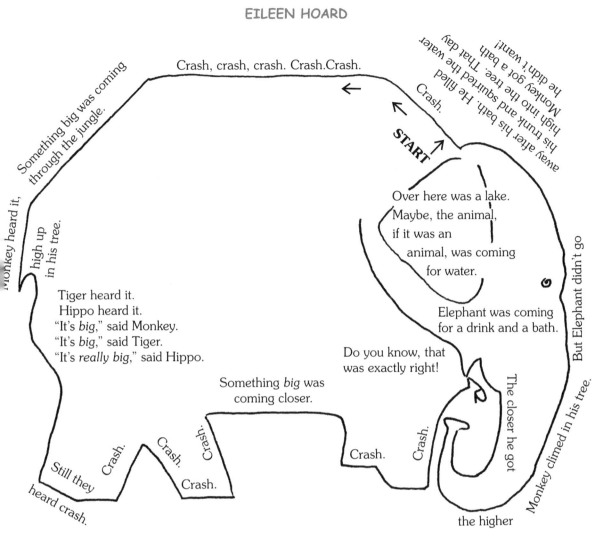

Crash, crash, crash. Crash. Crash.

Something big was coming through the jungle.

Monkey heard it, high up in his tree.

Tiger heard it.
Hippo heard it.
"It's *big*," said Monkey.
"It's *big*," said Tiger.
"It's *really big*," said Hippo.

Still they heard crash.

Crash. Crash. Crash. Crash.

Something *big* was coming closer.

Over here was a lake.
Maybe, the animal,
if it was an
animal, was coming
for water.

Elephant was coming for a drink and a bath.

Do you know, that was exactly right!

Crash. Crash.

The closer he got the higher Monkey climbed in his tree. But Elephant didn't go

away after his bath. He filled his trunk and squirted the water high into the tree. That day Monkey got a bath he didn't want!

Crash.

START

Crash, Crash, Crash
by Eileen Hoard

Crash, crash, crash.
Something big was coming
through the jungle.
Monkey heard it,
high up in his tree.
Tiger heard it.
Hippo heard it.
"It's *big*," said Monkey.
"It's *big*," said Tiger.
"It's *really big*," said Hippo.
Still they heard crash, crash,
crash, crash, crash!
Something big was
coming closer.
Over here was a lake.
Maybe, the animal, if it was an
animal, was coming for water.
Do you know, that was
exactly right!
Elephant was coming for a drink
and a bath. The closer he got
the higher Monkey climbed in
his tree. But Elephant didn't go
away after his bath. He filled
his trunk and squirted the water
high into the tree. That day
Monkey got a bath he didn't want!

Drawing Halloween Pictures

by Eileen Hoard

It was getting close to Halloween and some kids were drawing Halloween pictures.
#1 A little boy drew this. He said it was a bat.
#2 A little girl drew this. She said it was a cat sitting in a window.
#3 Another girl drew a ghost waving out a window.
#4 A bigger boy drew this and said it was a haunted house.
#5 Then he drew this and said it was a pumpkin patch.
#6 Well, I saw a clown coming out of the pumpkin patch carrying something heavy.

Do you know what it was?

You're RIGHT…a pumpkin (or a jack-o-lantern)!

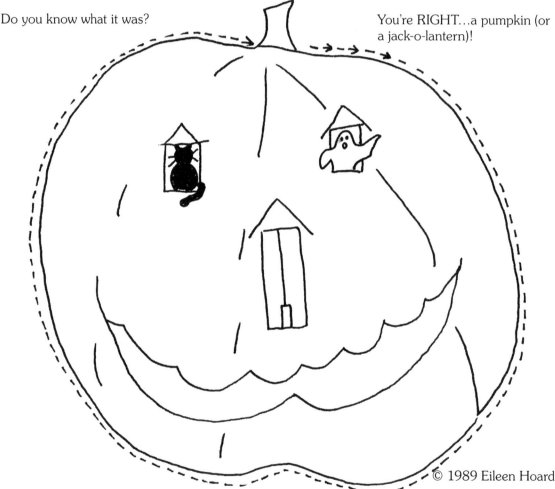

© 1989 Eileen Hoard

Use a black marker to draw #1, 2, 3 & 4.
Use a green marker to draw #5.
Use an orange marker to draw #6, the pumpkin outline.
Add the slash marks of the pumpkin skin.

Jamie's Surprise

by Eileen Hoard

Jamie was at the beach.
He found a stick. He stuck
it in the sand.

He ran around the beach
and found more and more
sticks. He stuck them all
near each other in the
sand.

He walked all the way
around his sticks. Then
he hopped all the way
around his sticks. Next he
sat down in the sand. He
had an idea. He drew in
the sand.

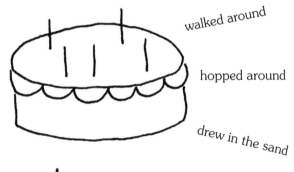

walked around

hopped around

drew in the sand

Someone began to sing
"Happy Birthday to you…"
And it was then that he
realized he'd made a
birthday cake!

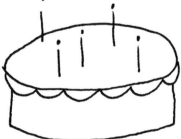

© 1999 Eileen Hoard

Mojo's Walk

Inspired by a Syd Hoff drawing

Story by Eileen Hoard

There was a little boy named Mojo.
He lived in the jungle. One day, as he
was walking on a path through the jungle
he saw footprints. He followed them. Then
the prints ended.

He heard something rustle.
He saw some bushes near the path.
Something was in the bushes!
He looked harder, but he could
only see…this.

He waited for 5 minutes and he looked again.
He saw something black.

All around him the grasses wiggled.

Suddenly, something moved and
he saw an eye.

Then the thing jumped at him and
growled "Roar!"

IT WAS A LION!

Mojo yelled, "GO away." That scared the lion
so much that he ran right off the page.

© 1992 Eileen Hoard

Natalie's Story

"By Natalie, age 10, who told me most of this story"...Eileen Hoard
Give the dog a name that will sound funny to that group.
It might be the name of the school, the teacher, or principal.

This is a man who has no arms.
He lost them in an accident.

He had a dog named _____.
His dog had fleas.

One day _____ got out and the
man chased him around in a circle.

He chased the dog up into the
mountains and into the hills.

Now, in these hills there were 2 caves.
In the caves lived 2 bears.

These bears loved to eat hot dogs.
When the man came across those
bears eating hot dogs he also found
his dog _____.

_____ was kind of a big dog
and he loved to eat hot dogs too.
He had brown spots on his sides and on
his tummy...and when he saw "His
Man" he wagged his tail.

.. and that is **Natalie's Story!**

mountains
caves
bears
hills
hot dogs
hot dogs

Talking to Grandpa

by Eileen Hoard

One day _____ was talking to her/his grand___ ___.
Grandpa asked, "Can ___
"Sure," said _____ and

"Can you draw a bigger o
"Sure," said _____, and
around the little circle.

"Can you draw a bigger one
"Sure," said _____, and drew a bigger circle
around the first two circles.

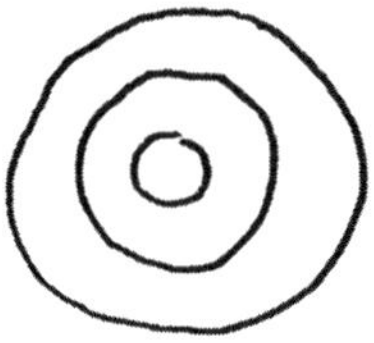

"Now you draw, Grandpa,
handed him the pencil/pe
"Sure," said Grandpa...and

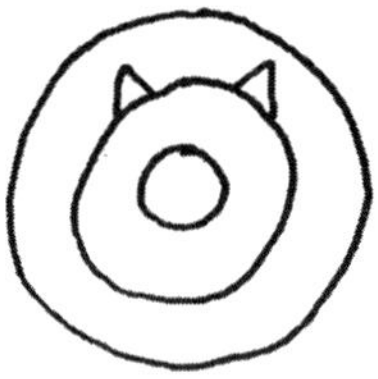

"Draw some more," said _____ and
Grandpa drew two feet.

"Can you draw more?" asked _____.
"Sure," said Grandpa and he drew two eyes,
two nostrils and a tail.
"Do you know what it is?" asked Grandpa.
"Sure," said _____. "It's a pig."

© 1999 Eileen Hoard

Thanksgiving Day Dinner

by Eileen Hoard

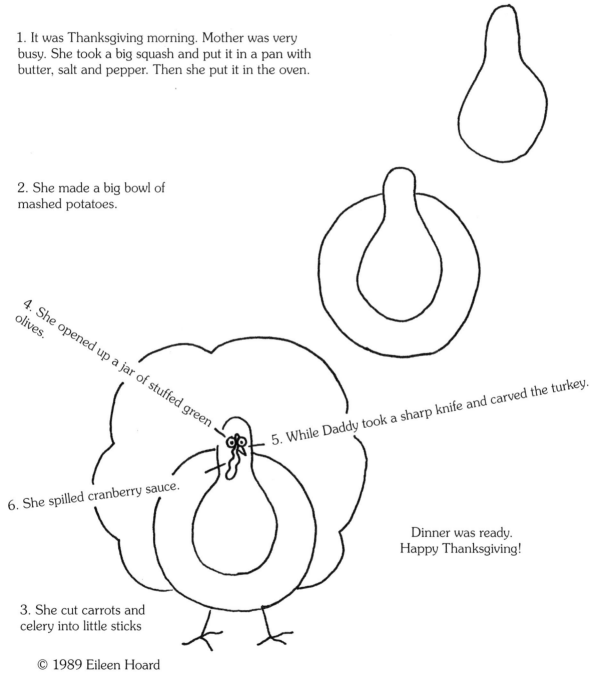

1. It was Thanksgiving morning. Mother was very busy. She took a big squash and put it in a pan with butter, salt and pepper. Then she put it in the oven.

2. She made a big bowl of mashed potatoes.

4. She opened up a jar of stuffed green olives.

5. While Daddy took a sharp knife and carved the turkey.

6. She spilled cranberry sauce.

Dinner was ready.
Happy Thanksgiving!

3. She cut carrots and celery into little sticks

© 1989 Eileen Hoard

The Very Busy Spider

by Eric Carle

Do not begin the story until you have drawn the fence.
If you have made a colorful cloth spider, put it on your hand before you begin to draw the web.

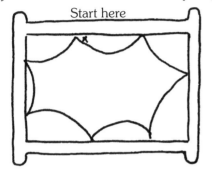

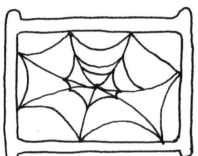

Continue drawing and finish the web as you recite the story.

Finally, as you say the fly has been caught, draw him on the web.

Be prepared for the children to "tell" the story with you! They know this one!

This Is My Picture

by Eileen Hoard

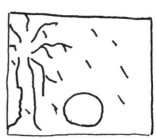

This is my picture. Can you guess what it is?

Yes! It's a snowstorm.

When it stopped snowing so hard I could see kids making something.

I could see this…

I could see this…

I could see this.

I could see this.
The kids' make another snowball. They put it on top.

They finished their snowman and they ran away to play.

But something began to happen.

I looked again and…

Oh, dear…the telephone rang. When I came back this is what I saw.

What happened?

I feel so appreciated when
I am telling stories.

- Eileen Hoard, Educator and Storyteller

Little Blue and Little Yellow was
first told as a drawn story.

- Vivian G. Paley

Chapter 9
PARTICIPATION STORIES

Going on a Lion Hunt by Harriet Ziefert
Let's Go Dinosaur Hunting by Andrea Brzezinski Breiling who "thought this up" in 1987 when
    she was nine years old
No Way José by Joe Hayes
Oh, Look by Patricia Polacco
Rain found in *Here Comes the Storyteller* by Joe Hayes
Rounding Up the Reindeer found in *Creative Activities for Special Education* by
    Sharen Metz Kokaska
Squeaky Old Bed found in *Crocodile! Crocodile! Stories Retold Around the World* by
    Barbara Baumgartner
The Earth Monster found in *Here Comes the Storyteller* by Joe Hayes
Who Will Save the Day? by Buff St. John in *Tempest Tossed: Poetry*
Z-Z-Zoink by Bernard Most

Participation stories are simply those stories which anticipate responses or movement by the children. Anyone who has ever gone to a preschool or a summer camp or taken part in Scouting has done a participation story. Can you remember slapping your thighs, then slapping them faster, clapping your hands, pantomiming excitement, exhaustion or fear? You might have pretended puffing up a hill or swimming in a river. When you got out of the water you looked around. What did you see? Maybe it was a bear! Then you had to turn, run and do all those actions in reverse until you were safely home and had slammed the door behind you! You were doing a participation story!

Going on a Lion Hunt features a little child who announces, "I'm going on a lion hunt." The child never leaves the backyard but encounters quicksand, a swamp, a cliff, a herd of toy elephants and finally a LARGE cat (the lion). Of course, the excitement of that unexpected confrontation demands a hurried trip back to the safety of the house! Similar excursions might involve looking for a bear, an elephant, a dragon, or a dinosaur. Creative solutions to getting past each obstacle exercise a group's imagination.

Let's Go Dinosaur Hunting came from my nine-year-old granddaughter's imagination. We had been reading *Dinosaur Days* by Liza Donnelly. Andrea thought it would make a good participation story. Here is her version.

Words	**Actions**
Let's go dinosaur hunting.	Slap thighs, slap, slap, clap slap.
Let's go dinosaur hunting.	
Let's go dinosaur hunting.	
Slip on your boots.	Pretend to slip on boots.
Open the door.	
Step outside and close the door.	Act out opening and closing the door.
Oh, oh there's lots of snow.	
We can't go under it.	Dip both hands as if to go under.
We can't go through it.	Motions as swimming.
We'll have to go on top of it.	
So, let's go dinosaur hunting.	Tap feet or slap legs.
Oh, oh look at this big pile of snow.	
It must be a bagaceratops, *for sure*!	
Let's uncover it.	Motion brushing off snow.
Oh, oh it's just a car.	
Let's go dinosaur hunting.	Repeat three times.
Oh, oh look at this big pile of snow.	
It must be a camptosaurus, for sure!	
Let's uncover it.	Motion brushing off snow.
Oh, oh it's just a bicycle.	
Let's go dinosaur hunting.	Repeat three times.
Oh, oh look at this big pile of snow.	
It must be a syntarsus, for sure!	
Let's uncover it.	Motion brushing off snow.
Oh, oh it's just a trash can.	
But let's go dinosaur hunting anyway.	
There's another big pile of snow.	
Let's uncover it.	Motion brushing off snow.
Oh No! It's a Dinosaur!	
Run! Past the trash can,	
past the bicycle,	Slapping thighs very fast.
past the car.	
There's your house…	
get the door open…	Act out opening and slamming door.
slam it shut!	
Pull of your boots.	Pretend to slip out of boots.
Let's look out the window and *see*	Pretend to look out window.
if we can *see* the dinosaur.	
Whew…it's gone!	Wipe brow with hand.
It's a good thing dinosaurs aren't REAL! FOR SURE!	

Another type of participation story requires the audience simply to participate verbally. *No Way, José* is the perfect example of this. Before you begin to tell the story you will enlist the help of the audience to say, "No way José!" whenever you give them the signal. A typical signal might be to point a finger at them. Other stories invite animal sounds at appropriate times. These kinds of stories keep your audience listening carefully for their opportunity to speak.

No Way, José will keep your audience's attention. Jose is a bossy little rooster who receives an invitation to the wedding of his Uncle Perico. On the way to the wedding he encounters a problem. Being a bossy rooster, he attempts to solve his problem by ordering *grass*, then *some sheep, a wolf, a dog* and *a man* to do as he bids. All refuse until he frightens the man into complying. The man chases the dog and the dog bites the wolf on the tail. The wolf jumps on the sheep, the sheep eat the grass and the grass goes swish-a-swish-a-swish, cleaning off Jose's beak as he ordered.

All through the story the audience says, "No way, José!" in response to his bossy requests. At the end the last laugh is on José. He assumes the family will want him to sing at the wedding. But the family says, "No way, José!"

You may find some similarity to the English cumulative tale *The Old Woman and Her Pig.* In this tale her pig will not go over a stile. She tries to enlist the help *of a dog, a stick, fire, water, an ox, a butcher, a rope, a rat, a cat* and finally *a cow.* Each action she requests is dependent upon another action to get the pig to go over the stile. P.S. The old woman does get home that night. You could tell this story as a participation story too. Think about the actions you could do!

Oh Look! The gate is open to the pen. Three little goats...
    "Can't go over it,
    Can't go under it,
    Can't go around it...
    But there's the gate and it's unlocked...
Squeak, squeak it goes as they go through it."
This is truly a brand new, classic, participation story as the wee goats "Click, click, click" their little hooves as they cross the bridge. Then they "Puff, Puff, Puff" as they climb the hill...and there's more! Finally at the fair, they see something that scares them so much that they hurriedly turn tail and head for home. All of their previous actions are repeated in reverse until they are safely home. The satisfying ending completes a beautifully illustrated story by Patricia Palocco.

Rain is another story from *Here Comes the Storyteller.* Frog needs help. It has not rained for a year and he feels he will die without some rain. Storyteller Joe Hayes enlists his audience in helping Frog and Locust sing their cry for rain. Locust says, "When one person works all alone he doesn't get much done. But when people work together, they can do a lot of work." This is a great story to encourage family or group cooperation!

Rounding Up the Reindeer provides the opportunity for both movement and sound. It is a charming participation story which includes Santa's walking, thundering, puffing, stepping, sliding on the ice and suddenly seeing a polar bear. But Santa was not successful in rounding up his reindeer. After he sees the polar bear he hurries home to safety. Once he is inside Mrs. Santa points to a surprise just outside the window. The reindeer have come!

Squeaky Old Bed, in Barbara Baumgartner's collection of stories from around the world, relies on voices for participation. It just begs little voices to cry, boo-hoo, bark, meow, squeak and oink.

When I tell it, I also use a dog toy that squeaks like the old bed. You may allow a child to do that part. It is a very easy story to learn because there is much repetition in the story line.

The Earth Monster "looked like a big, round pile of dirt…It had a mouth like a cave." As Coyote travels from village to village he hears frightened people talking about a monster who swallows entire villages. Since Coyote is so clever, he thinks he can be of help. He finds out what the monster is afraid of and he persuades the village people make all of the sounds. Encourage the audience to make all of the sounds, in unison, that frighten Earth Monster. The audience will roar, shake rattles, pretend to play drums and sing at the top of their voices! Earth Monster gives one last roar and **turns into stone**! But that is not all of the story. When you hear the rest of it you will know why the people called Coyote a great hero.

Who Will Save the Day? A ship named The Tempest Tossed has been out at sea for weeks. As Captain Wayward and his crew sail home they experience a few problems. This humorous participation story follows their adventures involving an iceberg, a hurricane, and a sandbar. However in the end they do dock safely at Boston Harbor and the whole crew sighs, "At last, at last!" This poem has hand actions for the refrain. You may want to teach these first. It will be easier for the children to join in right from the start.

Z-Z-Zoink by Bernard Most provides an opportunity for the audience to make a number of animal sounds that are repeated throughout the story. Listening for their cues will keep your audience attentive.

Children *love* participation stories, so be sure to learn at least a few of them to include in your storytelling sessions. They often offer the relief you need when the audience gets restless. To be a successful and sought-after presenter, vary the types of stories you offer an audience.

Shark's Dinner
Stevie draws lots of
sharks. Could this shark
tell us a story?

Art by Stephen Chandler, age 3.

Patience is necessary, and one cannot reap immediately where one has sown."

- Soren Kierkegaard, 1813-1855

*Be yourself,
the world worships the original.*

- Jean Cocteau, Writer

Chapter 10
STRING STORIES

When I tell string stories I always tell the children that moms, dads, grandmas, grandpas, aunts and uncles have told stories to their children long before there were books. I explain that one of the ways they told these stories included creating string figures as they spoke. Older children enjoy learning that this was one of the ways that earlier children learned about their tribe's history and rules. It was also, I inform the kids, how they and the adults of the tribe were entertained. Remember, I remind my audience, people haven't always had TVs, radios, iPods, CD players and computers to provide stories, music and entertainment.

String figures have a long history. String figures thrived from Alaska to Africa, from the Polynesian islands to Native American encampments. The same figure often had different names in different places. Many had no story attached. They were simply presented as finger games. Author and storyteller Anne Pellowski recommends string stories as a great way to get acquainted in other cultures whether or not one knows the language. Someone is sure to recognize what you are doing and may even introduce a new figure to you.

In one storytelling session I performed the *Mosquito/Fly* story. A mom listened with her young son. When I ended the session she came toward me. With tears in her eyes she asked if she could look at my string. Of course, I handed it to her. She then told me that her grandmother in Europe had told this story to her when she was a little girl. She had forgotten all about it until she heard me repeat it. Now, she wanted to tell it to her own four-year-old. Of course, by then, I had tears in my eyes. What a treasure to have rekindled her memory of a grandmother who told stories to entertain her little granddaughter. Similar events may happen to you too!

You must be well prepared to tell stories with string figures. It is best to practice the figure and the story separately until you have conquered both. Then you can practice doing them together, making the words and the actions fit. That is usually not too difficult. If you are doing a complicated part of the string figure and need to concentrate on that, feel free to stop talking for a few moments. You will find that even blasé adults are drawn to a demonstration of string games. I suspect this has always been true.

Since string figures each require different lengths of string, I use special colors which relate to each story. For example, brown works well for *The Farmer and His Yams* as does green for *Lizard and Snake*. Of course, I choose red to represent the dragon in *Pierre and the Dragon*. Be sure to note the length of string needed for each story and whether or not the ends are to be tied together.

I first found the following string figure in a book of simple magic tricks. I was looking for additional string stories to tell since the children enjoyed them so much. The main point of the trick involved threading a needle, so I built my story around that idea.

Old Lady and Her Animals

by Eileen Hoard (A String Story)

You will need:
> a slightly stiff string 30" long…Do not tie the ends together.
> a pair of silly glasses with cardboard lenses that look as if you could not possibly see
> anything through them

[Keep the string and the glasses out of sight until ready to use them in the story.]

This string trick was "… observed among the Omahas, the Pawnees and the Kwakiults; the Japanese and even in the Caroline Islanders." In addition, one hundred years ago anthropologist Dr. Boas recorded its use as a way for members of a Shaman Society to identify each other when they met in the forest.[1]

There was an old woman who lived in a
white house with a yellow straw roof. She
had a lot of pets. She had a gray mouse with a
long pink tail, a calico cat, a brown dog
with black spots and a black cow with white spots.

One day the animals all began to make a lot
of noise. The mouse squeaked, the cat meowed,
the dog barked, and the cow mooed. They all
wanted to go for a walk.

But the old woman's dress was torn. Since   [Pretend to reach up as if her
she had only one dress, she insisted she   sewing basket was on a shelf
sew it up before she went out of the house.   above your head.]
She got down her needle and thread.

She put on her glasses…   [Put on your glasses. Begin to wrap
since she didn't see too well any more.   string around your thumb.]

[Leave 9" of String A hanging down.
Then start with String A between
thumb and palm and wrap it
around the thumb three times.
Close thumb tightly to
hold string in place.]

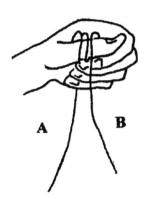

A   **B**

She tried to thread the needle and missed.

[Using String B, form a loop (eye of needle)
and push it under the thumb already holding
the string you wrapped around your left thumb.
Now, using the right hand, grasp the
end of String A and pretend to thread
the needle. Make two inaccurate attempts and
on try #3 pull the string up sharply
(still holding tightly to all the strings under
your left thumb). The string will
appear to go through the eye of the needle.
Try once to the left and once too high.]

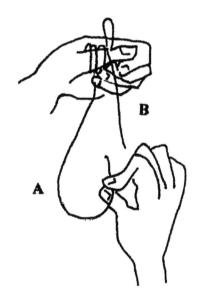

B

A

Then it looked like she missed…but the needle was
threaded. The animals didn't believe it. The
mouse squeaked, the cat meowed, the dog barked,
and the cow mooed. So the old woman unthreaded
the needle and did it again.

[Do the trick again for your audience.]

Then she sewed up her dress and took
her animals for a walk. Do you know, that from
that day to this, the animals still have *never*
figured out how she threaded her needle?

Once, when I was still looking for string stories, I tried weaving a loop of string on my fingers.
Soon, I developed a figure that I had not seen before. I liked the fact that, in the end, it fell freely
off the hand. Now that I had a figure, I found it easy to create a story. Following is the result.

Pierre and the Dragon

by Eileen Hoard (A String Story)

[You will need a string 50" long. Tie the ends to each other in a knot.]

Once upon a time in a land far, far away there lived a dragon.
Its home was in a cave near a lovely little town. In fact everything
in that lovely place was truly wonderful except that a dragon lived nearby.

Now, in this town there lived a little boy named Pierre. He and his mother
lived in a small house near the dragon's cave. His mother was terribly
afraid of the dragon so Pierre bravely told her, " I'll get rid of the
dragon for you, Mother."

In a shaky voice his mother croaked, "Oh, dear."
She worried constantly about her son, for Pierre had made many *silly* mistakes.
However, she didn't say anything more except, "Thank you, Pierre."

"I'll get going right now, Mama," said Pierre as he started off down the road.
Soon he met a cow.
"Have you seen the dragon?" he asked.
"I wouldn't be this calm if I had," said the cow.
Next, he came across a large horse standing in the middle of the road.
"Have you seen the dragon?" asked Pierre.
"Can't you tell?" questioned Horace the horse. "Look
at my lovely mane. It's all singed…dragon fire, you know."
"Phew, it smells awful," complained Pierre. "Which way did he go?"
"Which way did *who* go?" asked Horace. He was a really thick-headed horse.
"The dragon, The dragon!" yelled Pierre impatiently.
"Oh, *that* dragon," muttered the horse.
"Yes," hissed Pierre, "Which way?"
"That way!" neighed the horse, pointing his nose down the road.
Then he called after Pierre, "That dragon is a *girl* dragon, you know.
Her name is Elizabeth."
"A girl," moaned Pierre. "How long ago did you see her?"
Don't know," mumbled Horace. "Can't tell time."
Gee whiz!" wailed Pierre, "A girl dragon! They're the most dangerous kind."
But he went racing down the road just the same.
Suddenly he heard a scream.
A little girl yelled, "A dragon! A dragon! Help!"
Pierre ran fast. The screaming got louder and louder
and he ran faster and faster. Then he saw what was happening.
The dragon had the girl trapped up in a tree. Pierre knew *he*
would have to save her because no one else was around.

He thought a moment, then began to sing,
    "Dragon oh, dragon!
    I love you true.
    Come play with me.
    Do, do."

Elizabeth, the girl dragon, hesitated, then turned toward Pierre. She looked deep into his eyes as he sang,
    "Dragon oh, dragon!
    I love you true.
    Come play with me.
    Do, do."

He didn't love her, she could tell.
He had a big rock in his hand. He was her enemy.

Quick as a wink, Elizabeth pulled a
long piece of red rope out from under her
red wing. Quickly, she tied Pierre up.
He couldn't move. He was really scared!
He called for his mama. But she didn't answer.
The dragon was about to blow fire at him
when she heard someone calling,
"Elizabeth, Oh Elizabeth! Elizabeth, Dearest."
It was a huge, black dragon named Frank,
who was her mate. She forgot all about
the little girl. She forgot all about Pierre.
She ran to catch up with her big black dragon,
Frank, and off they flew to a land far away.

But Pierre was still tied up.

Elizabeth had tied him up very tightly. She had even
put in a few extra knots for good measure.
He used his mouth and loosened one of the cords.
Then he wiggled and wiggled until he was FREE.

Since Elizabeth the dragon had flown far away
Pierre's mother thought he was **a hero**!
The townspeople thought so too! They all
celebrated.

The little girl kissed him.
'Oh, yuck,' he thought. 'How embarrassing!'

Begin string figure here.

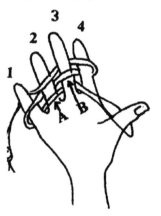

[Place 1 loop over the thumb.
Wind <u>double</u> string over
and under fingers as shown.
Slip bottom loops A & B over
fingers 2 & 3. With left hand
hold on to loose end of the
double cord. Slip thumb cord
off with teeth. Let go of the
double cord. Wiggle fingers
as if struggling. The string
will fall from the hand.]

But, that day and forever after, he got just about anything he wanted from his mom because the dragon was gone and she didn't think he was such a silly boy any more.

An excellent story is **Lost! A Story in String** by Paul Fleischman. Eight string figures are used to illustrate this story, the tale of a little girl lost in a blizzard. Each string figure builds on the one immediately prior. Accomplished finger artists will find this story a great way to display their skill. Directions and drawings for each figure are found at the end of the book. Eventually, the audience learns that a grandmother has actually told her own childhood story.

Finally, three of my all-time favorite string stories (included in almost every performance) are;

> *Farmer and His Yams*
> *Lizard and Snake*
> *Mosquito*

Please find these string stories in *Storyvine* by Anne Pellowski. They are not hard to learn and the directions are very clearly stated.

String figures are at once challenging and intriguing. Many children already do them. In fact, if *you* have any problems with a string figure, children may be one of your best troubleshooting resources! Enjoy the satisfaction of using one of the world's oldest visuals to help you tell stories to young children, their older siblings, and parents.

[1] Caroline Furness Jaynes, *String Figures and How to Make Them.*
(New York: Dover Publications Inc., 1962).

Chapter 11
QUILT STORIES

- How should quilts be used?
- Choosing a story you wish to represent on a quilt
- A list from my collection of quilt stories
- More quilt-story ideas and titles

Quilts that tell a story can become a constant companion for the child lucky enough to have one. Lying on or holding a soft quilt is a lovely tactile experience. Stories *are* everywhere, aren't they?

I am a storyteller. And, I am a quilter.
So of course, I *would* find a way to both 'quilt a story' and 'tell a quilt'.

I have two embroidered quilts from my childhood. One features six different animals while the other one is covered with embroidered bunnies. They were used to help me recognize animals and name them. Why not put a simple children's story on a small quilt top too? As I began to explore the choices, I found a number of books that told stories *about* quilts. While these are especially appropriate, many other stories can also be told on quilts.

In fact, here are several great quilt story possibilities.

Caps for Sale as told by Esphyr Slobodkina
The Clothesline and Other Quilt Stories by Six Friends (See Adult Resources)
The Crazy Quilt by Kristen Avery
It Looked Like Spilt Milk by Charles Shaw
The Keeping Quilt by Patricia Polacco
Luka's Quilt by Georgia Guback
Mrs. Noah's Patchwork Quilt by Janet Bolton
My Grandmother's Patchwork Quilt by Janet Bolton
Patchwork Folk Art by Janet Bolton
The Quiltmaker's Gift by Jeff Brumbeau
Quilt Story by Tony Johnston
The Rag Coat by Lauren Mills
Sweet Sarah and the Freedom Quilt by Deborah Hopkinson
Goldilocks and the Three Bears Traditional
The Three Little Pigs Traditional
Tortilla Quilt, Piñata Quilt & Tamale Quilt by Jane Tenorio-Coscarelli
Who's Under Grandma's Quilt? by Rachel Waterstone

How should quilts be used?

When I present to a group, I often tell a quilt story by holding up the quilt with the help of one other person. If there are just a few children, we all sit or lay on the floor around the quilt. Some people don't get it when I speak of the emotional charm of quilt stories. For me, they evoke strong feelings of being nurtured. It is also a very tactile approach to storytelling. Touching quilts seems to be a universal need. They just beg you to stroke them, feel them, and be embraced by them. If this holds no meaning for you, try touching and stroking a quilt, any quilt, and find for yourself the charm they hold.

One at a time, these and quilts like them, could be placed on the floor in front of bookshelves in a classroom or in a quiet corner. At home or at school quilts might hang on the wall or be rotated for snuggling at sleepy times. Encourage the children to retell the stories from the quilts. Cotton quilts are very sturdy and can be washed in the washing machine. Use them and enjoy them.

You allow a lot of audience interaction when you urge a group to help you tell a quilt story. There is always room for imagination and a variety of interpretations. The language can come from the children. Since their opportunities for expressive language are often limited, this medium provides an excellent opportunity for them to use their words. In addition, once the general outline of the story is established, the children will be able to tell a quilt story independently. They won't need you or an audience to recreate the events shown on the quilt top.

Choosing a story you wish to represent on a quilt

When choosing a story you wish to represent on a quilt top consider the following:
- Simple story with few characters
- Well-known story, so omitted details do not detract
- Easily represented characters

Ask yourself:
- How big will the quilt be?
- Is it more bother than it is worth?

(If you are an avid quilter probably no amount of work is too much. It you're a novice, you might start with something simple so you won't get burned out.)

A list from my collection of quilt stories

I first saw the **Caps for Sale** quilt in a magazine. While the story was not identified, the pictures on the quilt blocks told the tale. I recognized this quilt from India as Esphyr Slobodkina's story. This story has turned up in more than one culture. For this quilt I wrote the story out on a muslin square using a permanent marker. Then I attached it to the back of the quilt. That way, my story is always available for a quick refresher, if I need it. You can make this quilt of muslin. The pictures are drawn with permanent black marker. I used black fabric bars to separate the drawings. You can see this and two other quilts on page 122 of this book.

I have just found **The Clothesline and Other Quilt Stories**. It holds six delightful, colorful quilts, each with their own story.

The Crazy Quilt is a story by Kristen Avery. Without permission, Tanya Bear makes a crazy quilt of pieces cut from her family's favorite clothes. Oh, dear!

It Looked Like Spilt Milk is by Charles Shaw. Puffy clouds of different shapes make this a delightful story. It is easy to remember because of the repetitious line, "It looked like spilt milk. But it wasn't spilt milk, it was a ... (bunny, ice cream cone, tree, etc.)."

Patricia Polacco writes **The Keeping Quilt**. This is the story of how a quilt made from love and pieces of loved ones' old clothes traveled from Russia to the United States and was handed down for many generations.

Luka's Quilt is Georgia Guback's creation. Luka is disappointed with the traditional green and white Hawaiian quilt Grandma has made for her and Grandma feels sad. Luka does not like her new quilt. That changes things between them until Grandma figures out a way to make Luka's quilt bloom with color.

Mrs. Noah's Patchwork Quilt is by English author Janet Bolton. While the ark sails on rough water, Mrs. Noah's quilt grows as she pictures animal after animal surviving the great rain.

My Grandmother's Patchwork Quilt is also by Janet Bolton. Grandmother's memories of her life as a girl on the farm take form as figures are placed on the small quilt. When it was finished it made a warm quilt for her dolls.

Patchwork Quilt Art by Janet Bolton is a wonderful resource for doing quick quilts. Her technique could be used with any story you choose to represent. Both experienced quilters and those who have never made a quilt before will find it fun.

The Quiltmaker's Gift is by Jeff Brumbeau. This charming fable is about a quiltmaker who quilted with the colors of oceans, snow, wildflowers and sunsets and only gave her quilts to the poor. A king in the story is very rich but not at all happy. The quiltmaker teaches the king how to be happy by having him give away all of his riches. As he begins his transformation, she makes a dazzling quilt for him. Soon he becomes poor but declares himself to be, "the richest man I know."

Quilt Story is authored by Tony Johnston. A quilt made for Abigail is found in the attic where mouse, raccoon and cat have enjoyed it. When refurbished, it once again comforts a little girl.

The Rag Coat is told by Lauren Mills. Minna's patchwork coat is full of stories. The pieces tell of the people who once wore them. This is a warm coat full of warm family stories.

Sweet Clara and the Freedom Quilt by Deborah Hopkinson is a quilt with a story that could have come from our history. The imaginary Sarah is a slave living in the South. While wishing for freedom, she overhears traveling slaves speak of something called a map. They tell her a map could help her escape. Trained as a seamstress, and with access to thread and fabric scraps, Sarah gradually gains information about the roads, rivers, swamps and landmarks which will aid her escape. She incorporates this into an unusual new quilt pattern and follows her map to freedom. School-age children enjoy the telling of Sarah's story and often think you are showing them a quilt actually made by her. This story has been made into a quilt by Tonee White author and nationally known as a designer of unique quilts. You may write to her to inquire about her pattern for this attractive story quilt at 7644 E. Minnezona, Scottsdale, Arizona 85251.

More quilt-story ideas and titles

Alphabet motifs printed or embroidered can be made into quilts also. I have a Christmas alphabet that is a printed miniature quilt representing many symbols of the season. Nursery rhymes embroidered on squares and made into a quilt allow little ones to learn the rhymes with the visual cues on the quilt top.

Traditional stories such as **The Three Little Pigs** or **Goldilocks and the Three Bears** also make dear quilts and provide pleasant childhood memories.

Tortilla Quilt, Piñata Quilt, and **Tamale Quilt** are written and illustrated by Jane Tenorio-Coscarelli. Coscarelli's three stories all end with a child receiving a new quilt representing the story.

Who's Under Grandma's Quilt? is by author Rachel Waterstone. "I'm telling Grandma," said Piglet. "You'd better not touch Grandma's quilt." But the curious animals found out who was under that quilt. This is a story even young ones can act out.

I'll continue to look for quilt stories....Will you?

When I was about four years old the neighbor's baby died and all the women was called in to help. Mama knew what her part was because right away she took some blue silk out of her hope chest. I remember that silk so well because it was special and I got to carry it. When we got to the neighbors some of the women was cooking and the men was making the casket. Mama and three other women set up the frame and quilted all day. First they quilted the lining for the casket, and then they made a tiny little quilt out of the blue silk to cover the baby.

- The Quilters by Patricia Cooper and Norma Bradley Allen

Chapter 12
"HOLD ON YOUR LAP" STORIES

If you've never heard of "Hold on Your Lap Stories" that's understandable. I simply call some of my visuals "Hold on Your Lap Stories" because that's what one does with them. For me, this kind of storytelling developed gradually. I now love to present them and I constantly seek more story lines that can be represented by something held on the storyteller's lap. These stories stand out as a unique category. They are not felt board stories, story wheels or quilts. They are different from string stories, drawn stories or paper stories. So, to me, they are "Hold on Your Lap" stories. Following is a story list with brief comments on each.

Alligator Baby by Robert Munsch
A Pizza the Size of the Sun from the book *A Pizza the Size of the Sun* by Jack Prelutsky
Baby Rattlesnake found in *And It Is Still That Way* by Byrd Baylor
A Big Fat Pie by Pat Edwards
Big Mac by Cindy Hoard and Eileen Hoard
Fly's Castle found in *15 Easy Folktale Fingerplays* by Bill Gordah
Goldilocks and the Three Bears is often considered a traditional story. But it may have been an
    original by Robert Southey or may have been rewritten between 1834 and 1837.
Good Night Gorilla by Peggy Rathmann
If You Give a Mouse a Cookie by Laura Numeroff
Magic Spoon found in *Jar of Fools* by Eric Kimmel
My Little Sister Ate One Hare by Bill Grossman
Piggy Pie originally in *Mudluscious as Pomeroy Pig*, adapted by Eileen Hoard
Sylvester and the Magic Pebble by William Steig
The Doorbell Rang by Pat Hutchins
The Gingerbread Boy is a modern version of the old folktale, *The Pancake*.
    It was originally printed in *St. Nicholas Magazine* in May 1875.
The Hungry Thing by Jan Slepian
The Lost Button found in *Frog and Toad Are Friends* by Arnold Lobel
The Mitten an old Russian tale with many authors and artists, one version by Alvin Tresslet
The Three Bears Meet the Three Blind Mice by Eileen Hoard (see Chapter 17 for the story)
The Very Bare Polar Bear found in *The Animals' Merry Christmas*
The Water Cup found in *The Family Storytelling Handbook* by Anne Pellowski as told by
    Ruth Stotter

Alligator Baby

Robert Munsch's stories are hilarious and this one is no exception. Mom and Dad bring home the wrong, new baby until Big Sister Kristen takes over and brings home a "people baby" instead of a "zoo baby". While telling this story, hold a quilted blanket in the crook of your arm. Inside the blanket you have hidden felt figures of the animals Mom and Dad bring home instead of their own new baby. Directions and patterns are found at the end of this chapter.

A Pizza the Size of the Sun

This is really an entertaining poem about making a pizza. While telling it, give the children all the topping pieces: vegetables, pepperoni pieces, cheese and sauce. Explain that they are to put their pieces on the muslin pizza dough when you mention them in the poem. You might start with the round circle of dough in the pizza box. If it is set in the center of the floor all the children can gather around it. You may need to tell this more than once to satisfy your little pizza lovers.

Note: Some felt pieces go home in little pockets but you can quickly make replacements.

These are the directions for making the muslin pizza round.

To make *A Pizza the Size of the Sun* you need to:
> Cut out two 14" circles of muslin.
> Sew them together…leaving a space open the width of your hand.
> Turn the 'dough' inside out.

Cut a piece of batting just slightly smaller than a 14" circle and put into the 'dough'. You can machine sew the 'dough' and stuffing all together at the same time if you choose. You can lay a narrow roll of 'crust' inside your 'dough' before you sew the finished 'dough' shut. Next, tack the batting in place with some small hand stitches.

Provide a 14" pizza box from a pizza parlor. Store your pizza pieces in it. Glue a copy of the poem inside the lid so you will have it when you need it.

Cut sauce, red pepper pieces, tomato wedges and bits of pimento from red felt (three sheets). I cut three pieces of 'sauce' to overlap on the crust.

Cut three big cheese pieces and mushrooms from a warm beige felt (three sheets).

Cut pepperoni slices from brown felt (3/4 sheet).

Cut olive slices from black felt (1/4 sheet).

Cut green pepper slices from dark green felt (1/3 sheet).

Cut yellow pepper slices from dark yellow felt (1/3 sheet).

Cut peas from apple green felt (1/4 sheet). Use two small cookie size pieces of netting and glue peas and pimento between the pieces of net. Make three or more of these pieces.

Your "wonderful pizza the size of the sun" is now ready!!

Baby Rattlesnake

Holding a brightly colored, 7", soft, cotton, dog toy shaped like a snake is a good way to tell this story. The story is an Aesop-like American Indian tale of why Baby Rattlesnake was given rattles. The source, *And It Is Still That Way* is a book of stories collected from Native American children. The stories were told to them by their elders and often end with, "and it is still that way". While the cloth snake is not scary, it does hold the children's attention. The source of my particular snake is Fat Cat, Inc., Cracker Series, designed by Anne Lika. However, it would be easy to make a small snake of any cotton fabric or felt.

A Big Fat Pie

'I'm making a pie, a big fat pie," said the witch to a pumpkin rolling by. Then she popped it into her pie. Oh, my goodness! It could sound scary but it's not. As you tell this story the pieces are put into the pie. Right up to the end…but…Oh, I can't tell you that part! I do guarantee that you and the children will enjoy this story. Shall I mention the words 'poetic justice'?

Here's what you need to do to prepare:
>Cover a 2" deep aluminum foil coffee cake pan with tan felt.
>Hand sew or glue the sides to the bottom.
>Cut a cardboard circle large enough to make a top for the pie.
>Cut two felt pieces just 1/4" bigger than the cardboard circle.
>Put some padding between the two felt circles of felt.
>Sew or glue the pieces of the top together.
>The bottom and the top make your pie.
>(Note that the top is not fastened to the bottom of the pie.)
>Now you need a pumpkin, a black cat, a ghost and a witch hat.
>Make simple flat cut-outs of these felt shapes or, if you'd prefer,
>you can stuff the figures that you need. In any case
>they must fit into your pie.

>Keep the pumpkin, black cat, ghost, and witch hat in a pocket while you tell the story or set them beside you in a basket.

Big Mac

You need a hamburger made of felt wrapped in blue and white checked cloth to tell this rhyme. I have included the story in both English and Spanish as well as patterns for pieces needed. This is a pattern story which means the words follow a repeated pattern.

Big Mac begins with,
>'Blue wrapper, blue wrapper what do you see?
>I see a brown bun looking at me.
>Brown bun, brown bun what do you see?
>I see orange cheese looking at me.
>Orange cheese, orange cheese what do you see?'

The burger, pickles, lettuce, mustard, ketchup, onion, etc. can be stacked in the bun in any order. Tell it according to what you see. The adult may hold everything or the pieces can be distributed to the children each of whom will hold up their part when it is mentioned. That piece can then be added to the sandwich. *Big Mac* might be put into a book corner in a basket. Encourage the children to retell it. You may have noted that the story pattern is very similar to *Brown Bear, Brown Bear What Do You See?* by Bill Martin.

Fly's Castle

I like this Russian tale in which the fun is in the piling up of six 1-1/4" blocks, on which you Modge Podge pictures and words. The repeated lines and the surprise when you suddenly knock those blocks over make this a charming story. As you tell the story, pile the blocks. Then, when the last animal, the bear, arrives, you or a child can become the bear and with a swipe of your 'paw' knock over all of the blocks. During the story, the dialogue you glue to the backside of the blocks will help you keep track of the story. See the end of this chapter for directions and patterns.

Goldilocks and the Three Bears

Tell this old tale with a reversible doll. When you turn the Goldilocks doll over, the Three Bears are under her skirt. This cute little doll really does hold the attention of a group. They are very surprised when you turn her over and they see that the Three Bears have been quietly hiding under her skirt. The small added surprise of the family of bears makes it fun to tell this familiar story.

Good Night Gorilla

This dear little book is perfect any time, but is especially nice for bedtime. The zookeeper is saying "Good Night" to all of the animals. Then, something funny happens. You'll see that the colors of the keys are important if you are matching them to the pictures in the book. The children are often sticklers about this, demanding that you use the right key. If you are doing this story with a group, you may want to take the keys off of the key ring and allow each child to come forward with the correct key when it is used in the story. Someone might also hold the key ring as the keys are added back on to it.

This is almost a story without words, so write your own script. After hearing this story children will often say, "Tell it again." Directions to make the keys are found at the end of this chapter.

If You Give a Mouse a Cookie

Do you know this popular story? To create a visual you need only fill a box with items that move the story from beginning to end. I'll tell you about each one as it is listed.

> The cookie is made from play dough.
> Milk is just a plastic glass. Drop in some white acrylic paint and swirl it around to coat the glass so that it looks half full. Let it dry. You now have an instant glass of milk.
> You also need a napkin, a pen, a crayon, some paper to draw on, a small book, a rag for clean up, and small scissors. All of these can be real items.
> Further, you need a small bed, a blanket, and a pillow. I made mine from a kitchen matchbox and some fabric scraps.
> A friend actually peeled the label from a can of cleanser to make that item for me. Then she glued it to a cardboard cylinder to create a can of cleanser. No need to get that specific. Any fake label glued down on a cylinder will do.
> The broom was easy to make from a stick or dowel. I tied short lengths of raffia, cut to resemble bristles, to the broom handle and wrapped it with a piece of wire.

All of this needs to fit into a shoebox, providing ease as you hold all on your lap. This is another tale the children will want to try telling themselves as they take each item out of the box.

Magic Spoon

This story is a Jewish version of *Stone Soup*. You may want to use the spoon and a bowl when you reveal this story. While you don't need a pattern for this visual, you do need a wooden spoon of any size, a paintbrush, and bright acrylic paints. **GO WILD** when you paint your magic spoon! Swirls, dots, and question marks all look magical, as do clouds, moons, stars and squiggly lines.

Be sure to ask questions after telling this whopper of a tale. Some might include:

> Who provided the ingredients (onions, oil, potatoes etc.) used to make the latkes?
> Who brought the eggs? (oil, onions, flour, potatoes)
> What did _____ (name any character here) bring?
> Did the stranger bring anything?
> What did the townspeople offer the stranger for his spoon?
> Did the stranger trick the townspeople? How?
> So, is this spoon really magic? What makes you think so/not?

My Little Sister Ate One Hare

This is a story told in rhyme which makes it easier to learn. Because the rhyme in this story is so perfect, I learned it word for word. All items Little Sister eats are recounted with comic descriptions. The storyteller keeps repeating "We thought she'd throw up then and there, but she didn't!" She didn't, until she ate those peas.

I tell this story holding an oval basket which seems to hold a little girl. Whenever she eats something I add the same to my basket. The story ends with… "Eating healthy foods like these (peas) makes her sick, I guess. Oh, my goodness, what a mess!" At that point I happily scatter the contents of the basket all over the immediate audience. It's just great! Instantly I hear squeals, giggles and, "Oh, my gosh!" Then, of course, as the noise subsides we are all on a hunt to find every last piece, so that we can tell it again. Hobby and party stores as well as The Oriental Trading Co. are good sources for most of the edibles you need. The ants are so small that I glued them between two pieces of fine white net to keep from losing them. You can make the basket look like a doll is in the basket or you could just fasten a doll into the basket and add the things she eats on top of her. As long as the doll doesn't fall out when she 'throws up' you will obtain the same effect. You can see a photo of Little Sister on page 126.

Piggie Pie

This is a Thanksgiving story. Sitting in the barn, Piggie is very lonely and very hungry. He wishes his human family would share some of their dinner with him. The visuals for this story consist of: a tin pie pan, 2 apples, 2 pickles, a turkey leg, 2 slices of bread, and a piece of pumpkin pie. During most of the story you hold only the pie tin on your lap. As the family finishes eating, all of these leftovers are put into his pie tin. You can hide the food in your pockets or have it sitting beside you (half hidden) in a basket. I made most of the food in a sort of faux Paper Maché technique. Crunch up paper and compact it until you have a sturdy shape for each of the foods listed. Cover with the appropriate color of tissue paper. Wrap each food with the same color of sewing thread for stability. Paint each piece with three or four or coats of Modge Podge. This liquid is used for decoupage and is found in most craft stores.

Use cardboard to shape the slice of pie and cover with tissue or felt. I used tissue over the cardboard for the pumpkin and felt to cover the crust. If tissue paper is used, Modge Podge it well. The two slices of bread may be found in specialty stores or as pretend food in toy sections of larger stores. The bread is made of sponge, shaped like slices of bread. You could also use real slices of bread. Paper Maché food holds up quite well. I have my original pieces which are at least five or six years old.

Sylvester and the Magic Pebble

This is a very easy story to tell, especially with a wonderful Sylvester puppet. When you turn it inside out you are holding the rock that Sylvester turned into when he wished the lion would not eat him. If you don't have that puppet to help with the telling, use a piece of red glass or a small stone painted red. That is the color of the magic pebble Sylvester owned.

The Doorbell Rang

Mother bakes cookies and the two kids are dividing them up when the doorbell rings. Every time a new guest arrives the cookies are divided again. Soon there is only one cookie left for each child present. Then the doorbell rings again. How can they share their cookies once more? Mother opens the door to find it is Grandma with a whole plate of fresh cookies for the family.

A friend made a generous plate of play dough cookies for me so that the children could act out this story. I use red plastic plates to serve the cookies and allow the division of cookies. You might also use napkins. My experience is that at the end you'd better have real cookies available or even adults will be disappointed. I once presented this story at an afternoon teacher's workshop and I thought they would kill me when I did not have fresh chocolate chip cookies for them to eat.

The Gingerbread Boy

Tell this story with one fox or coyote puppet and a cardboard or wood gingerbread boy. Hold the gingerbread boy in one hand as he runs away from the little old woman and the little old man calling, "I can run away from you, I can I can." Use a puppet with a mouth that opens. March the cookie up the wolf's back, onto his neck, up on top of his head, and onto his nose. Grasp the gingerbread boy in the mouth of the puppet. If the cookie is small enough, it will appear to be swallowed by the wolf. GULP!

The Lost Button

Toad has lost a button off of his jacket. His friend, Frog, volunteers to help him find it. They go for a walk looking for the button and while they do find buttons, none of them are Toad's. To see how this story ends you'll have to look in the book.

To tell this story I use a small tin box that holds a variety of buttons. Some candies come in small, colorful, tin boxes. That's the kind I like to use. The collection of buttons includes different sizes and different shapes of buttons. Make sure to have some buttons which have two holes and some with four holes. I rarely tell the story with exactly the same buttons that I used the last time. I have collected some unusual buttons that make the story even more interesting.

The Mitten

I told you about this story earlier. I did it as I began my career as a storyteller. Here then, are the patterns for my version of The Mitten. (See the end of this chapter).

The Three Bears Meet the Three Blind Mice

This is a story that I tell while holding three small bears dressed in Halloween costumes. You will find this story in Chapter 17.

The Very Bare Polar Bear

This is a genuinely gentle Christmas story. It is not about getting lots of presents. Instead the polar bear wants to be of help to Santa. Santa needs help to get everything done. The solution is for the elves to take over Santa's tasks in the stores and on the street corners. They are soon dressed in Santa's old suits but they have no beards! Oh, dear! Can you guess what happens? What do they do for beards? Does Santa get everything done in time for Christmas? Mr. Polar Bear knows the answer to all of these questions. You will love this story.

This story requires one, stuffed, white polar bear and two smaller white baby bears. You will also need red felt for a simple red suit for Daddy Bear and his two baby bears.

My pattern may not fit your bears if they are of a different size but you'll get the general idea of how to cut out these easy suits. When you read the story you will find out why you need them. The patterns are found at the end of this chapter.

The Water Cup

Present this sentimental tale while holding an old cup or mug. I use my father's silver baby cup which is now over one hundred years old. Of course, read the story before you try to tell it. Note: (1) Put 1" of water in your cup before your audience arrives. (2) You will end up spilling the water all down your front. You know ahead of time that you are going to play a joke on yourself, but the audience is totally surprised, you are wet, and a good time is had by all!

Acting out any story can be easy. If the children are not very verbal, one teacher can read the story while the children with props act out what is being read or told. Keeping props to a minimum aids in success. There is little stress on the kids, except to listen, and of course the peer audience will tell them what to do and how to do it if they hesitate. Be familiar with any story before asking children to act it out.

ALLIGATOR BABY

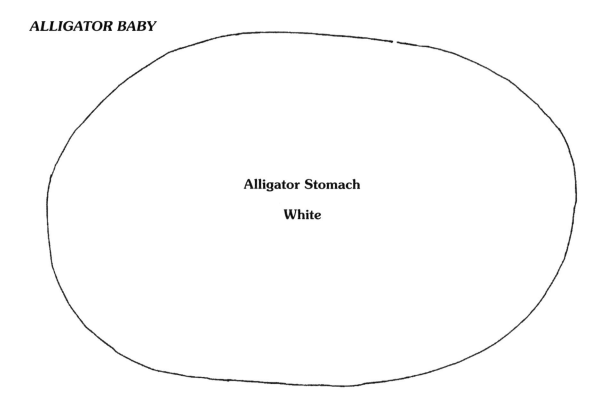

Alligator Stomach

White

Buy a piece of quilted fabric 15" x 20" for this little quilt. Turn each edge under one inch by hand or on the sewing machine. Put the animals and baby figures in the blanket in the order they are needed:

Alligator will be on top.
Under him is the Seal.
Below Seal will be Monkey.
Last comes the "people baby".

All will be on the right hand side of the quilt.

The thickness and firmness of the little quilt will help to support the felt animals. Place felt animals on the right half of the quilt with tail, arms and legs folded up out of the way so they cannot be seen by the audience. When the left side of the quilt is placed over the right side, the animals are hidden. As the story proceeds, you can pull out little arms, legs and tails without opening the quilt. This is why it is so important to put the animals into the quilt in the correct order.

ALLIGATOR BABY

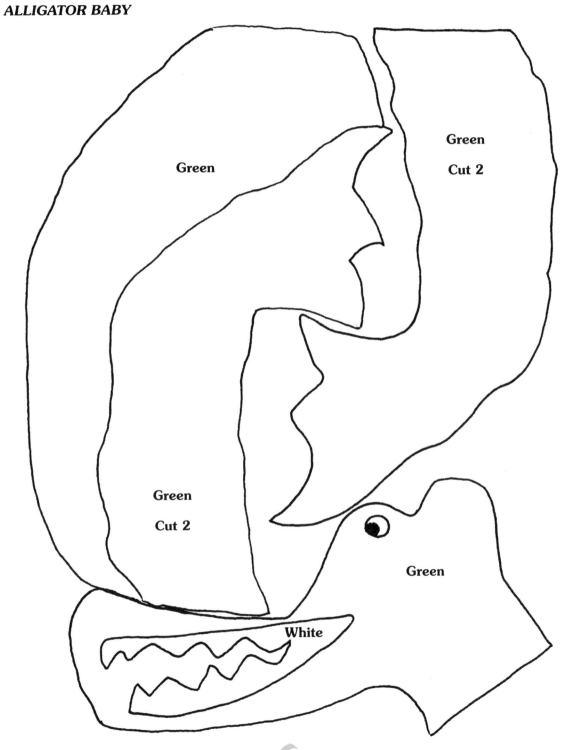

Green

Green

Cut 2

Green

Cut 2

Green

White

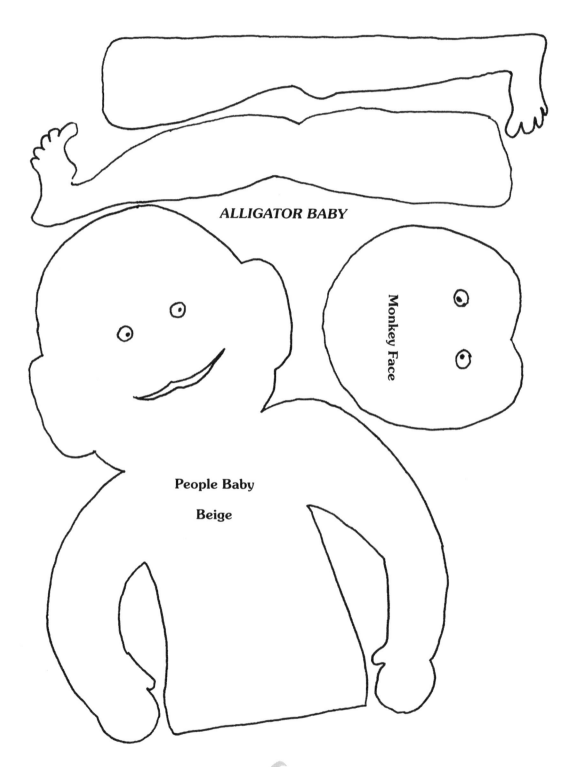

ALLIGATOR BABY

Monkey Face

People Baby

Beige

ALLIGATOR BABY

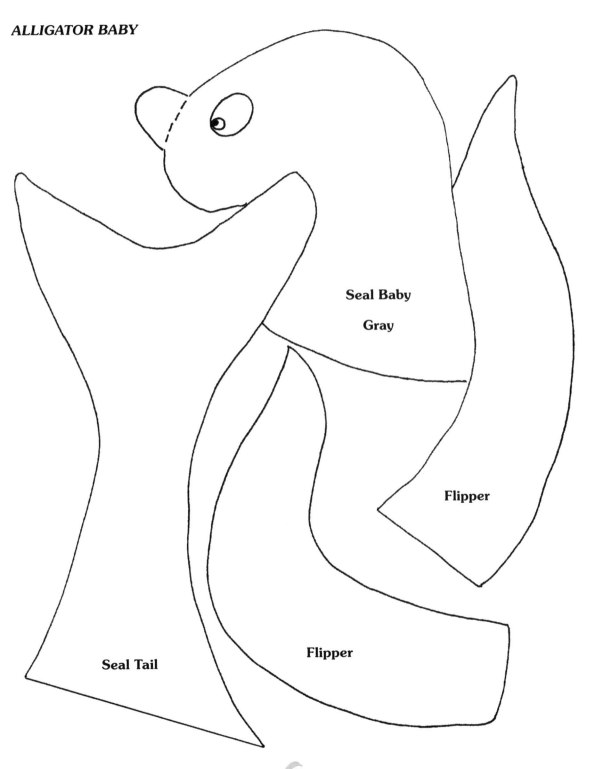

Seal Baby

Gray

Flipper

Flipper

Seal Tail

ALLIGATOR BABY

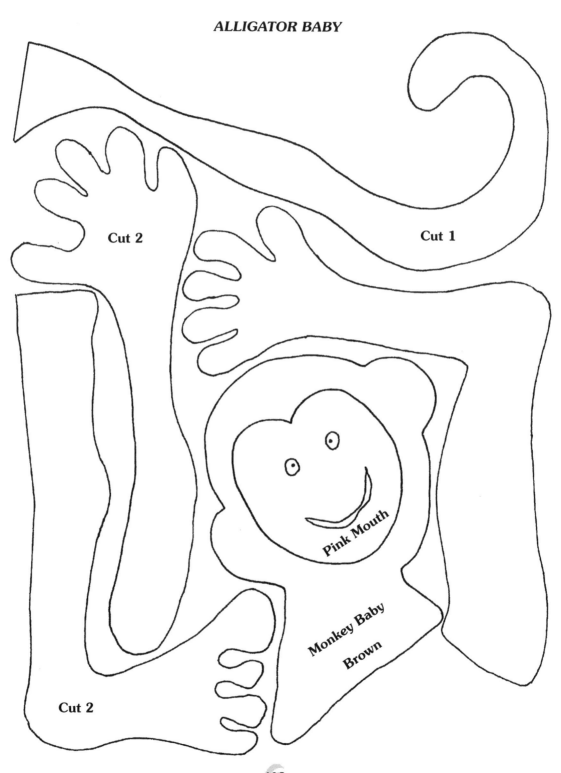

Cut 2

Cut 1

Pink Mouth

Monkey Baby

Brown

Cut 2

BIG MAC

Cut out the following:
    Pickles, Ketchup, Lettuce, Mustard,
    Cheese is 1/4 sheet of felt
    2 Black Burger pieces, 2 Tan Bun & 2 White Bun pieces
    1 Purple Onion, 1 Lavender Onion

Burger: Use black or brown thread to sew the two burger
    pieces together and leave a few inches unstitched.
    Use a running stitch. Put a small amount of batting
    in the burger. Finish stitching to close. Next, sew back
    and forth across the hamburger.

Buns: Use beige thread to sew a running stitch around the Tan
    buns to gather slightly. Put some batting in the little 'cup'.
    Lay these 'cups' on the White bun pieces. Use a
    Running stitch to sew the Tan and White
    buns together.

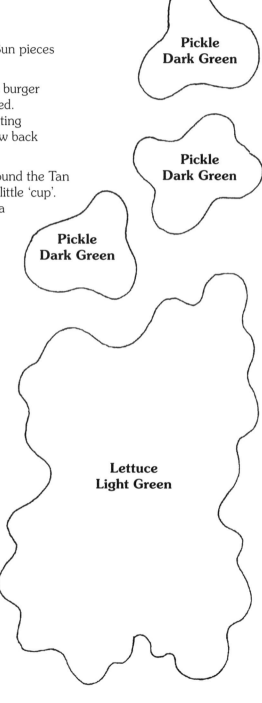

**Pickle
Dark Green**

**Pickle
Dark Green**

**Pickle
Dark Green**

**Lettuce
Light Green**

BIG MAC

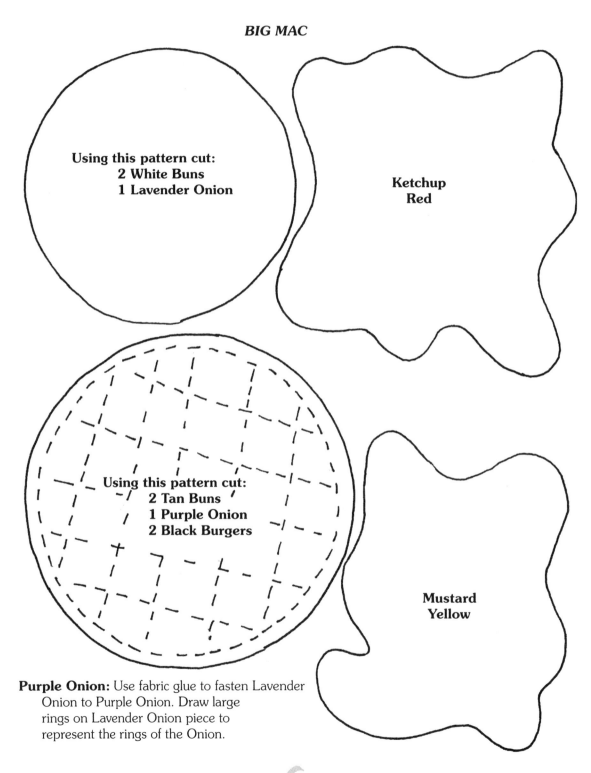

Using this pattern cut:
2 White Buns
1 Lavender Onion

Ketchup
Red

Using this pattern cut:
2 Tan Buns
1 Purple Onion
2 Black Burgers

Mustard
Yellow

Purple Onion: Use fabric glue to fasten Lavender Onion to Purple Onion. Draw large rings on Lavender Onion piece to represent the rings of the Onion.

BIG MAC

Blue Wrapper, Blue Wrapper what do you see?
I see a Brown Bun looking at me.
Brown Bun, Brown Bun what do you see?
I see Red Ketchup looking at me.
Red Ketchup, Red Ketchup what do you see?
I see Yellow Mustard looking at me.
Yellow Mustard, Yellow Mustard what do you see?
I see Purple Onion looking at me.
Purple Onion, Purple Onion what do you see?
I see Orange Cheese looking at me.
Orange Cheese, Orange Cheese what do you see?
I see a Black Burger looking at me.
Black Burger, Black Burger what do you see?
I see Green Pickles looking at me.
Green Pickles, Green Pickles what do you see?
I see a Brown Bun looking at me.
Brown Bun, Brown Bun what do you see?

I see a Big Mac looking at me!

The story above is said in a rhyming fashion like the story *Brown Bear, Brown Bear What DO You See?*, with each child holding one of the pieces listed above.

UN CUENTO DE BIG MAC

Papel azul, papel azul, que miras tu?
Yo veo pan café mirandome a mi.
Pan café, pan café, que miras tu?
Yo veo lechuga verde mirandome a mi.
Lechuga verde, lechuga verde, que miras tu?
Yo veo salsa roja mirandome a mi.
Salsa roja, salsa roja, que miras tu?
Yo veo mostaza amarilla mirandome a mi.
Mostaza amarilla, mostaza amarilla, que miras tu?
Yo veo cebolla morada mirandome a mi.
Cebolla morada, cebolla morada, que miras tu?
Yo veo queso anaranjado mirandome a mi.
Queso anaranjado, queso anaranjado, que miras tu?
Yo veo hamburguesa negra mirandome a mi.
Hamburguesa negra, hamburguesa negra, que miras tu?
Yo veo pepinos verdes mirandome a mi.
Pepinos verdes, pepinos verdes, que miras tu?
Yo veo pan café mirandome a mi.
Pan café, pan café, que miras tu?

Yo veo un BIG MAC mirandome a mi!

FLY'S CASTLE

Supplies needed:
Copy of drawings and words
6 wood 1-1/4" blocks
White acrylic paint
Modge Podge available at Craft Stores
Paintbrush
Crayons
Waxed paper
Scissors

See patterns and photos (p.123)

Directions:
- Paint blocks white on all sides.
- Allow to dry.
- Use crayons to color the animal pictures (colored markers will run if you apply Modge Podge).
- Cut out animal pictures (which follow) as small squares.
- Apply Modge Podge to one block and put one animal on it.
- Do the same with each of the other blocks.
- Cut out the words in small squares as you did the animals.
- Match the words to the correct animal and apply to the opposite side of the block. You will only use two sides of each block.
- Continue to apply coats of Modge Podge (4 or 5) to permanently attach paper pieces to the block. Allow to dry between coats.
- Store the blocks in a Ziplock bag along with the story. This will make it easy to locate when you are ready to tell it the next time.

FLY'S CASTLE

A folktale from Russia
Adapted from Fly's Castle found in 15 Easy Folktales by Bill Gorah

 **"I",
said
the fly.**

 **"And me!"
called
the flea.**

 **"Me too!"
cried the
mouse.**

 **"Ya-hoo!"
said the
hare.**

 **"I'm here,"
cried the
fox.**

 **"Here,
here,"
wailed
the wolf.**

To present this story, let individual children build the block tower (castle). Start when the fly is mentioned by the storyteller. Add each animal block to the tower as it is mentioned. Choose one child to be the bear. As the story finally unfolds…the bear's paw swipes down the tower.

For once it is _acceptable_ to knock down a tower of blocks!!!
How delicious!!!

GOODNIGHT GORILLA

To make pipe cleaner keys you will need:

One each of long pipe cleaners:

Red	**Green**	**White**	**Blue**	
Purple	**Black**	**Yellow**	**Pink**	**Orange**

Cut   Cut

Cut   Cut

Bend small wires around the body
of the key to create prongs on the key

Crimp pipe cleaner ends down very firmly so that
no one may be poked with a sharp end of wire.

Hang each key on a nickel-plated steel ring
which opens up and snaps shut. These may be
purchased at office supply stores.

PIGGY PIE

Adapted by Eileen Hoard from the original source *Mudluscious*

It was Thanksgiving Day and Pomeroy Pig could smell all kinds of good smells coming from the house. Then more family started arriving carrying more good things to eat. Aunt Sally brought a big jar of homemade pickles. She loved to make big green pickles. Uncle Fred carried a big bowl of shiny red apples. He had picked them from trees in his own backyard. Grandma's basket held three freshly baked pumpkin pies. Grandpa was holding hot bread he had baked himself. He loved to bake bread in his new bread maker.

Pomeroy Pig checked his pan...nothing there. Pomeroy peeked in the window of the house. He saw the children setting the table. They put on knives, forks, spoons, plates, napkins, glasses and even a decoration for the center of the table. It was Thanksgiving after all. Next, the children put the chairs around the table. He could see Dad in the kitchen carving the turkey and Mother making mashed potatoes and gravy. He checked his pan again...it was still empty. He peeked in the window once more and saw everyone at the table pigging out! But, no one came to feed him. Pomeroy Pig felt sad. He curled up in a corner of the barn and pouted.

In the house, the family finished dinner and began to clear the table. Finally, Pomeroy would get his dinner.

      "Oh, look," said Aunt Sally. "Two pickles left."
      "Nobody ate this turkey leg," said Uncle Fred.
      "Two slices of my good bread left," said Grandpa.
      "One piece of pumpkin pie," said Dad.
      "Pomeroy likes apples for dinner," said Jason.
      "I know," said Mother, "I'm sure he thinks we've forgotten him. I'll take this out to him so he can 'pig out' too!!!"
      Pomeroy Pig ate up every bit of it!
      "Boy," he said, "I'm glad I'm a pig!"

Note: Add the leftover food to Pomeroy's pan as it is named in the story.

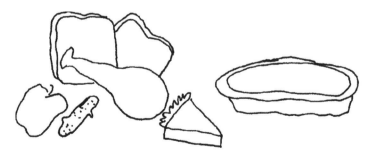

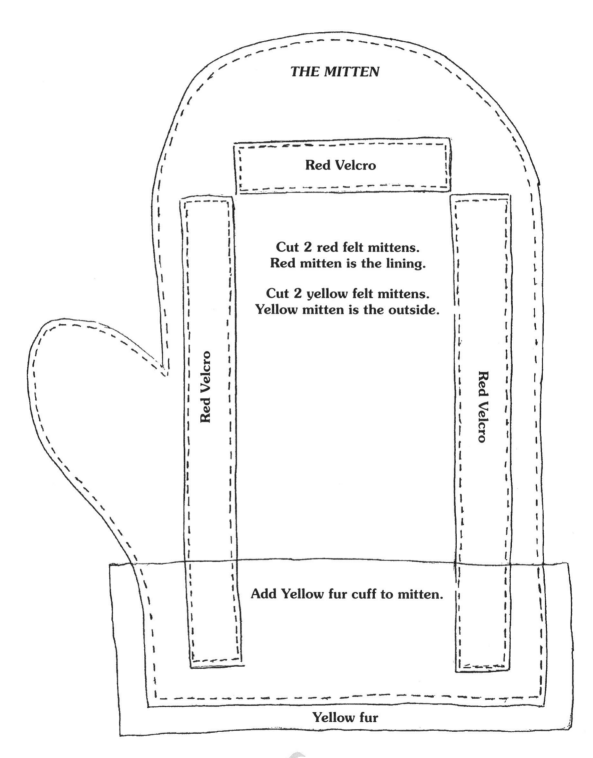

THE MITTEN

Red Velcro

Cut **2** red felt mittens.
Red mitten is the lining.

Cut **2** yellow felt mittens.
Yellow mitten is the outside.

Red Velcro

Red Velcro

Add Yellow fur cuff to mitten.

Yellow fur

THE MITTEN

THE VERY BARE POLAR BEAR

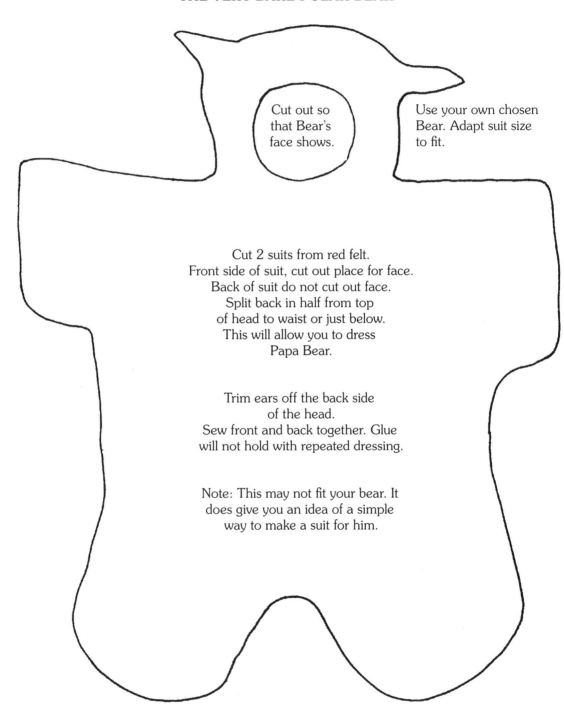

Cut out so that Bear's face shows.

Use your own chosen Bear. Adapt suit size to fit.

Cut 2 suits from red felt.
Front side of suit, cut out place for face.
Back of suit do not cut out face.
Split back in half from top
of head to waist or just below.
This will allow you to dress
Papa Bear.

Trim ears off the back side
of the head.
Sew front and back together. Glue
will not hold with repeated dressing.

Note: This may not fit your bear. It
does give you an idea of a simple
way to make a suit for him.

THE VERY BARE POLAR BEAR

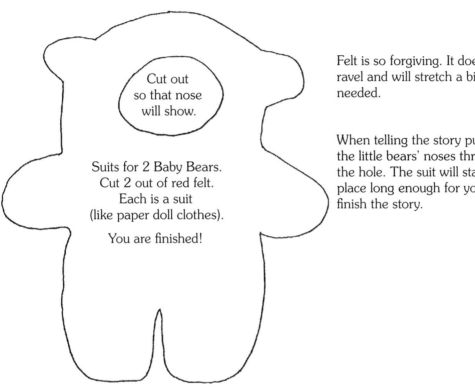

Cut out
so that nose
will show.

Suits for 2 Baby Bears.
Cut 2 out of red felt.
Each is a suit
(like paper doll clothes).

You are finished!

Felt is so forgiving. It doesn't ravel and will stretch a bit if needed.

When telling the story put the little bears' noses through the hole. The suit will stay in place long enough for you to finish the story.

Ice Cream Cone Scoopers

This story offers a colorful way to help Paul taste
and eat a super big ice cream cone.
Slurp, slurp, slurp!
Paul wanted as many flavors as he could get on his cone.

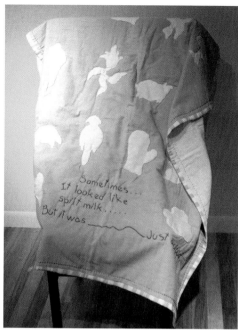

It Looked Like Spilt Milk
It did look like spilt milk, a mitten, a bird, etc. But it was "just a cloud". Even the youngest can tell this rhyme with the quilt as a guide.

Sweet Clara and the Freedom Quilt
The quilt becomes a map to freedom via streams, ponds, roads and the Ohio River. Follow the North Star.

Caps for Sale
This durable old tale comes to us on a quilt from India. The pictures tell the story of monkeys who stole the vendor's caps.

Alligator Baby
Other baby animals arrive home when Mom and Dad are supposed to be bringing home a new "people baby". It takes Big Sister to solve this problem and get the real new baby safely home. Hold all of the babies in a small quilt while telling this funny story.

The Mitten
This old Russian tale is the story of a lost mitten that keeps a number of animals warm. Stuffed inside the cozy mitten, they are comfortable until a tiny, old, black cricket wiggles in. Too full, the mitten breaks wide open and drops all the animals in the snow.

I'm Making a Pizza the Size of the Sun
Let the children help tell this story by having them add the sauce, cheese and all of the other toppings to this life-size 14" pizza. Keep it in a real pizza box and put a copy of the poem in the lid to remind the storyteller of the exact wording.

Fly's Castle

This castle is built of six blocks piled upon each other. Each block introduces a new animal to the listeners. Words on the back of the block keep the storyteller on track with the story. Fly built a castle for herself and invited a few friends to "Come on in." All is well until a big bear arrives. A swipe of his paw makes the blocks tumble down. Of course, a child can knock the blocks over.

The Very Bare Polar Bear

Polar bear gave Santa's helpers all of his fur to make beards. He got so cold that Mrs. Santa made him a lovely red suit to keep him warm. His little boys got cozy suits, too.

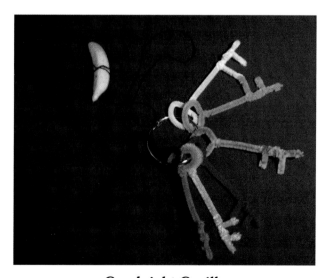

Goodnight Gorilla

Hold these colorful keys as you tell about how Little Gorilla opens the cages of the animals at the Zoo. When the animals are free, a funny thing happens. Mouse always makes sure Little Gorilla has his favorite snack, a banana.

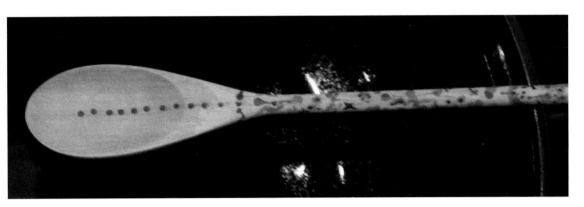

Magic Spoon
Paint this magic spoon to help tell this old Jewish tale about making latkes.

A Big Fat Pie
What a curious way to make a pie.
The little witch put in a cat, a ghost and a pumpkin.

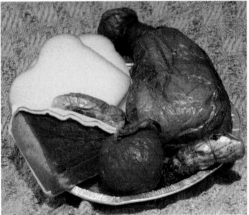

Piggie Pie
Piggie is really hungry.
After Thanksgiving dinner, he finally
finds yummy food in his tin.

My Little Sister Ate One Hare
She will eat all of this stuff too. When she finally eats some peas...
She...Oh my goodness! What a mess!

Gingerbread Boy
Make an old story a lot more exciting. The wolf puppet seems to be swallowing the gingerbread boy.

Big Mac
You can almost eat this felt hamburger. Lots of colors to recognize and an easy story pattern make this visual a hit with lil' kids.

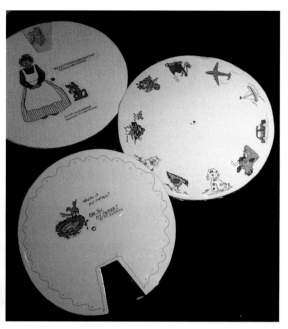

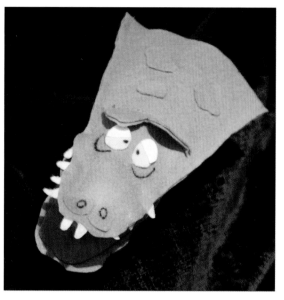

Story Wheels
Turn the top wheel to display the next
character to the audience.
(Note the unassembled wheel for working
understanding.)

Mr. Frimdimpny
joins the story ***Don't Make Me Laugh.***
If you make him laugh, you will have to
go back to the beginning.

I Went Walking
Each animal is led to recognize the next. It's even fun for shy little ones to hold paddles.

Platypus' Hat
Corks bounce and set the stage
for a whimsical session
of storytelling.

Pail Story
Write your own story and
pull it out of the pail to
delight your audience.

Story Apron
Fill a carpenter's apron with
your story accessories. Kids will
wonder WHAT is inside.

Imagination is not a blast from on high, it is a whisper in an ordinary room.

- Chase Collins, creator of Bedtime Tales

Chapter 13
STORY WHEELS AND PADDLE STORIES

How Old Mother Hubbard's Dog Finally Got Dinner found in *Mudluscious*
Are You My Mother? by P.D. Eastman
Have You Got My Purr? by Judy West
The Cookie Mystery by Tammy Zimmerman
Old MacDonald Had a Woodshop by Lisa Shulman
Henny-Penny an English Fairy Tale
It Looked Like Spilt Milk by Charles Shaw
I Went Walking by Sue Williams

STORY WHEELS

The idea of the story wheel came to me from the book *Mudluscious*. A story wheel is a piece of round cardboard with pictures attached to help tell a story. On top of the first cardboard round sits another round with a wedge cut out of it. As the storyteller turns the top around, pictures are revealed one at a time. This helps the children to interact with the story. It also assists in telling and recalling the story.

Story wheels are quite simple to make. You will need:
- One fresh 12" round cake card board (available at small bakeries or party stores)
- One piece of tag board or other thin card board 12" in diameter
- Pictures to put on the wheel (hand drawn or cut from magazines)
- One paper fastener, scissors and glue or a glue stick

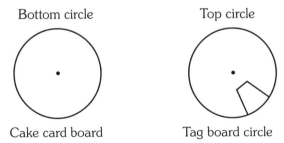

Bottom circle   Top circle

Cake card board   Tag board circle

Directions:
- At the center of each of the rounds create a small hole with a very small screwdriver or an ice pick.
- Cut a wedge out of the tag board circle (see pattern). When this circle is placed on top of the cake card board, all should be able to see one picture at a time as the story is told.

- Now, arrange the pictures in order carefully on the cake round so that each one can be seen through the wedge in the top tagboard circle without revealing parts of other images.
- Glue the pictures to the cake round. If you have words or pictures to glue to front or back of the story wheel, do that now. Let pictures dry.
- Put in the paper fastener.

You have made your own story wheel!

Postscript Suggestions:
- Laminate the two wheels. Separate them before laminating. Laminate both to provide longer life. If you don't have access to a laminator, cover them with clear Contact paper or take them to a copy store to have them laminated.
- For convenience, glue a copy of the story to the back of the story wheel. Decorate the front with title and drawings.

At the beginning of this chapter I listed stories which lend themselves to story wheels or paddles. As you begin to see how successful paddles and story wheels are, you and the children may choose to write some new stories to tell in this manner.

Following are descriptions of several stories that are effective as story wheels or paddle stories.

How Old Mother Hubbard's Dog Finally Got Dinner
Old Mother Hubbard was on her way to the store to get some food for her dog. On the way she forgot what she was going to get. She asked each animal she met, "What do doggies like to eat?" The pig said, "Corn." The bird said, "Worms" and the little boy said, "Pizza!" Old Mother Hubbard was not satisfied with the answers she got until she met Mama Dog. Of course, Mama Dog told her, "Dogs like bones." The audience easily interacts as you turn the story wheel to show each new answer. The children will enjoy retelling this easy story on their own.

Are You My Mother?
This is an old favorite of young children. As soon as he is born, a young bird begins to look for his mother. He asks a number of animals, "Are you my mother?" Since he asks a cat, a dog and a cow the answer is always, "No, I'm not your mother." He tries asking a car and a plane with no luck. He asks a bulldozer too. In the end, the bulldozer re-deposits him in his nest just as his mother arrives with a juicy worm. Since young children do worry about getting separated from Mother, this story both entertains and satisfies.

Have You Got My Purr?
A little kitten thinks she has lost her purr. She questions many animals asking, "Do you have my purr?" No one has her purr but each does have its own sound. Finally, Owl suggests she go back and ask her mother about it and, of course, Mother Cat is able to help. There is plenty of opportunity for audience participation as the animals announce their own sounds. The children identify the pictures of the animals as the kitten asks them about her purr. It is the 'purrfect' story pattern for a story wheel.

The Cookie Mystery
(Written during a teacher workshop and also found in Chapter 17.) In this story a sweet lady tries to find out who left a big chocolate chip cookie on her doorstep. As she tries to solve this mystery

she meets her mailman, the florist, and other friends. She asks each one whether they know who baked the cookie. No one knows where the cookie came from. Then she gets a great idea. Each night she makes a big cookie to deliver to a different neighbor, thereby sharing an enjoyable surprise with each. It is obvious why a pattern story such as this works well on a story wheel.

Old Mac Donald Had a Woodshop

Old Mac Donald had a SHOP. E-I-E-I-O. And in this shop she had a SAW. E-I-E-I-O. With a ZZTT ZZTT here and a ZZTT ZZTT there…"

What a hoot this is. This can be a story wheel or a paddle story. There is a unique sound connected to each tool. Sing this book or tell it. The tune for *"Old Mc Donald had a Farm"* works very well. You'll be repeating the sounds and naming the tools over and over. In this book Old Mac Donald is a W-O-M-A-N. It is a very pleasant, learning, singing, laughing experience.

To create a story wheel for *Old MacDonald Had a Woodshop*, cut pictures from a tool catalog to represent tools Old MacDonald uses in her woodshop. It is great fun!

Henny-Penny

Whether you call this story 'Henny-Penny', 'Chicken-Little', 'Chicken-Licken' or the 'Hare Who Ran Away' it is a beast tale that is cumulative and repetitive. One day while she was pecking at corn in the farmyard, something hit Henny-Penny on the head…Whack!

Goodness me!" she said, "I must go and tell the king that the sky is falling." So she went along and went along until she met Cocky-Locky. She told Cocky-Locky, "The sky is-a-falling." Their conversation and those that follow with Ducky-Daddles, Goosey-Poosey, and Turkey-Lurkey all revolve around going to tell the king that the sky is falling. As one might guess, meeting with the next animal, Foxy-Woxy, is something different. Foxy-Woxy is a sly old fox who only wants to eat all the other animals. He tricks and eats all of them but Henny-Penny. She, by the way, never manages to tell the king that, "The sky is-a-falling." Instead, she runs away to hide from Foxy-Woxy. This old English tale makes a great felt board, story wheel or paddle story.

It Looked Like Spilt Milk

"It looked like a bunny, but it wasn't a bunny."
"It looked like an angel, but it wasn't an angel."
"It looked like a tree, but it wasn't a tree."
"It looked like spilt milk, but it wasn't spilt milk."
"It was just…a cloud." There are plenty more lines like this.

Very simple lines and lots of fluffy clouds in a blue, blue sky make this a story to remember.

Story wheels make wonderful additions to book corners. Once the children have heard the story they are able to tell it all by themselves. As the story wheel is turned the pictures remind them of what happens next.

PADDLE STORIES

A paddle story consists of paper plate paddles with tongue depressor handles. Each paddle represents one character of the story. Most of the stories with which you might use a story wheel will also work very well as paddle stories. While the story is being told have the children stand in front of the group and hold up their paddle. This will allow the whole group to interact with the story without any demand that they speak on cue. The whole audience may give responses. Children with paddles speak only if they want to. Even the shyest child is willing, often eager, to hold a paddle and stand in front of the group as the story progresses. Preschool teachers seem to especially enjoy this concept because it is so forgiving and lends itself to many concepts and stories.

Paddles are easy to make. Purchase small, sturdy, paper plates from a restaurant supply. You will also need tongue depressors for each paddle's handle.

For each paddle use:
- one paper plate (6-3/4" dessert or snack size)
- one tongue depressor
- tacky glue
- scissors
- appropriate pictures
- crayons or markers
- a plastic bag

Directions:
- Assemble your pictures and color them if needed.
- Cut out the pictures.
- Glue one to each paper plate.
- Glue the tongue depressor handle on back of plate.
  (Check to see that your pictures are right side up as you hold the handle.)
- Let dry thoroughly.
- Store in large plastic bag.

Because these paddles are much easier to store without handles, I asked teachers whether they would prefer these without. They state that children enjoy holding something by a handle. Do whatever you like!

I Went Walking

The first time I made story paddles it was for this book. The pattern of this story is,
> "I went walking."
> "What did you see?"

The child who is walking encounters one animal after another. This pattern lends itself to many subjects. You might create a new title, such as:
> I Looked in My Refrigerator
> I Went Driving
> I Went to the Grocery Store

and the story continues, "What did you see?"

The story pattern is incredibly simple and the possibilities are endless. It also becomes interactive when the children contribute responses. This could also be played without paddles as a game in the car or in the classroom.

Whether you use story wheels or paddles you actively include the children in your presentation. That increases their willingness to sit and to listen without disturbing others. They may not always be quiet, but they will be more likely to respond appropriately to questions related to the story. When they feel they can be successful, they are usually willing to provide answers aloud. Barriers to participation that can be broken down in early childhood will open doors for more positive elementary and secondary school experiences.

Following are the patterns/designs for the aforementioned stories. Feel free to reproduce or use as springboards for your own creations.

If you enjoy a story, if you really have a personal affection
for it, the odds are very strong that your listener will
enter into the spirit of the story with you and enjoy it too.
- Jack Maguire, Writer & Storyteller

I think the creative process is not about creating something else;
it's about the process itself creating who I am.
- Mayumi Oda, Writer

Instead of thinking about where you are, think about where you want to be.
It takes twenty years of hard work to become an overnight success.
- Diana Rankin, Writer

11

Are You My Mother?
by P.D. Eastman
drawings by Eileen Hoard
(for story wheel)
Glue title and fig. #11
on the top circle.

1

2

These figures are to be
colored and cut out. Glue
them in numerical order,
around the edge of the
cake round.
Consult directions at the
end of this chapter.

4

5

6

7

8

9

10

© 1998 Eileen Hoard

These figures are numbered for order as the story is told.

These figures are to be colored, cut out and glued around the edge of the cake round. See directions.

How Old Mother Hubbard's Dog Finally Got Dinner
Source of original story:
Mudluscious
Drawings by Eileen Hoard

Title of the story, Mother Hubbard and her dog are to be glued on the top circle of the story wheel.

1
2
3
4
5
6
7
8
9
10

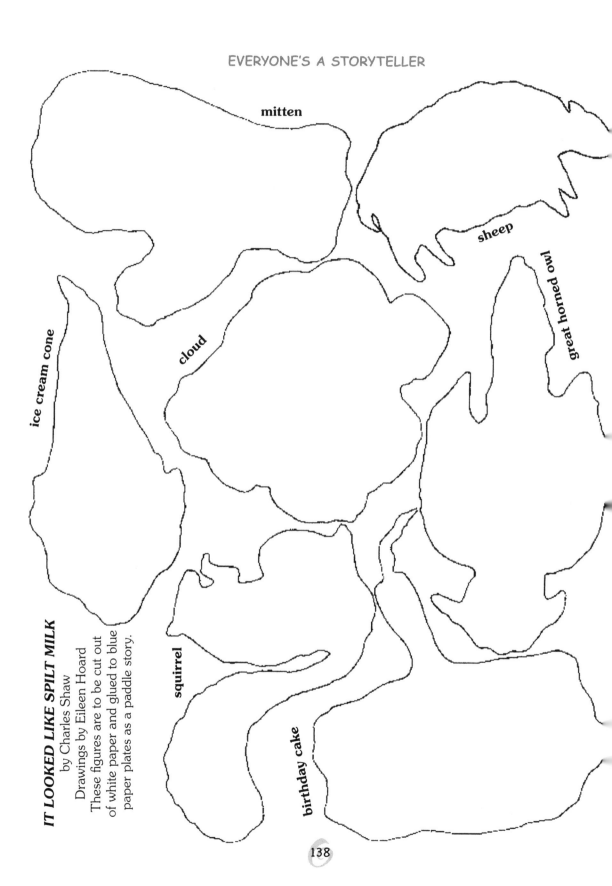

mitten

sheep

great horned owl

ice cream cone

cloud

squirrel

birthday cake

IT LOOKED LIKE SPILT MILK
by Charles Shaw
Drawings by Eileen Hoard
These figures are to be cut out
of white paper and glued to blue
paper plates as a paddle story.

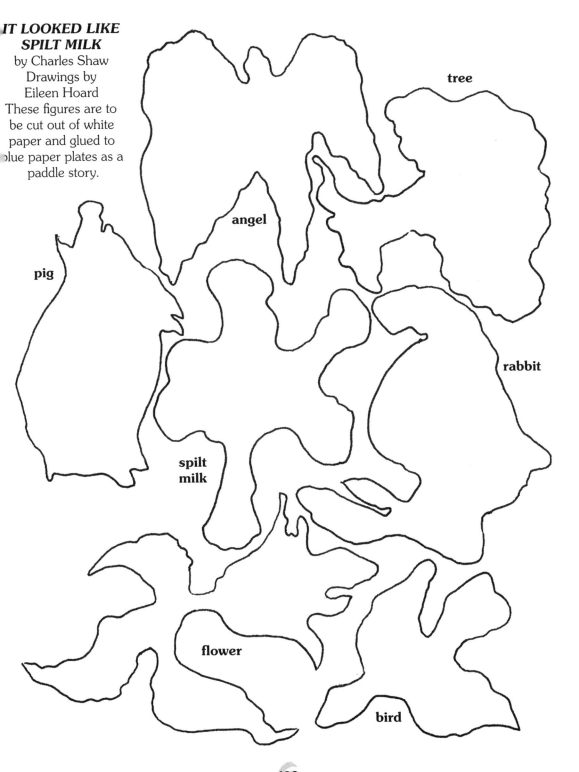

IT LOOKED LIKE SPILT MILK
by Charles Shaw
Drawings by
Eileen Hoard
These figures are to
be cut out of white
paper and glued to
blue paper plates as a
paddle story.

tree

angel

pig

rabbit

spilt
milk

flower

bird

I WENT WALKING
by Sue Williams
Drawings by Eileen Hoard

These figures are to be colored, and cut out of white paper, and glued to blue paper plates as a paddle story.

Chapter 14
STORIES WITHOUT PROPS (WELL ALMOST)

Don't Make Me Laugh by James Stevenson
The Greedy Old Fat Man by Paul Galdone
Many Moons by James Thurber
Wombat Stew by Marcia Vaughan
Pail Stories (see explanation)
Hat Stories (see explanation)

These stories, without significant props, do not fit easily into other categories, each holding its own promise of unusual storytelling possibilities. When you find a story that you like, float it around in your mind for a few days and, most likely, some distinctive idea will occur to you. Magically, you have a new way to tell that story. You may have a story on hold for months, awaiting a visual. Then, one day, the absolutely perfect idea will arrive. This process becomes part of your journey as a storyteller...enjoy it!

Don't Make Me Laugh is a book by the master of childhood humor. One five-year-old I know pronounces it "a hilarious book". Mr. Frumdimpny is in charge in this story! He makes the rules. His main rule is, "Don't make me laugh!" If you break this rule you must go back to the beginning of the story. Of course there are funny things that happen and you *WILL LAUGH!* I have included a pattern for a simple hand puppet to use as you tell the story or you may have a child manipulate it as the story is being told (see photo on page 126).

The Greedy Old Fat Man by Paul Galdone is a form of the old story *Fat Cat*. I first heard this story told by my friend, Cindy Pratt, from the bookshop. She dressed up in a large brown cape and a battered old hat. As she told the story, she gradually invited the characters to get under her cape. "We are pretending," she explained, "that the greedy old fat man has eaten you." [One thing I always do is ask the teachers to pick which children will go under the cape for the first telling. Those known to be shy or easily frightened may be ready for a turn after they actually see what will happen.] The cape expanded and expanded as the greedy old fat man ate more and more. At last, as he jumped from tree to tree chasing a squirrel, he fell and broke wide open. Of course, all of the animals he had eaten ran free.

"I'm out," said the dog.
"I'm out," said the cat.
"We're out," said the six little bunnies.
"I'm out too because I was never in," said the squirrel.

The repetitious lines in this story encourage energetic audience participation. It is a favorite with the children. You may always tell this tale more than once to accommodate the whole group.

Many Moons which won the 1944 Caldecott award, was James Thurber's first book for children. Although Thurber was famous as a humorist, this story is more of a fairy tale. A sick, little princess wants her father to get the moon for her. The king consults many of his great wise men. They are no help. Many speeches are given by them as they try to avoid the king's wrath. These humorous speeches can be difficult to learn.

I envision these men standing before the king with long pieces of paper in their hands detailing lists of all of their service to the king. My solution to getting through this story was to read from adding machine tape holding the lengthy speeches. Using this visual I did not need to learn all of those funny speeches. I maintained the humor Thurber had created and was able to tell this charming story wherein the Court Jester and Princess Lenore solve the problem with childlike reasoning.

Wombat Stew has a bit of music in it. It is a song Dingo, an Australian dog, sings as he dances around the fire. He thinks he is making wombat stew. His friends, Platypus, Old Blue Tongue Lizard, Echidna and Koala come to help. What I love most about this story is the scruffy leather hat Platypus wears. I wear such a hat with wine corks hanging from the brim. It is genuinely unique. The corks swing and bounce as Old Blue Tongue Lizard, Echidna, and Koala all add ingredients to the stew. Dingo stirs the pot, singing,

> "Wombat stew,
> Wombat stew,
> Gooey, brewy,
> Yummy, chewy,
> Wombat stew!"

There is music in the back of the book, or make up your own tune. In the end, with the help of the other animals, Wombat gets away and Dingo gets his come-up-ance. It is very Australian and very funny! If you can do an Australian accent so much the better.

Pail Stories

First, find a small pail. Use any size you like. Mine is only about two and one half inches tall. Next, you need a length of adding machine tape long enough to allow you to write a short story. Make it up yourself or use one you have read. Jokes work well also. Add drawings if you like. It is fine for them to be very elementary. When you are finished, roll up the tape so that it will fit into the pail. When you bring the pail out no one can see what is in it. Or, if they can see the paper, they don't know what is on it.

As you tell the story, unroll the paper. The story in the pail can be changed often to keep up the mystery. Or, you may put a small item which represents a different story, into the pail. Here is the first story I made up:

> I saw a little girl walking along the beach carrying a pail.
> As she came by I looked in the pail. I saw some shells and a small fish swimming in a few inches of water at the bottom of the pail.
> The fish spoke to me. "My name is Joe."
> "Hello Joe," I said.
> He looked at me and asked me my three favorite colors.
> I told him red, yellow and green.
> Then he said I could ask for three gifts…one red, one yellow and one green.
> So I asked for red glasses, yellow feathers and green plants.
> Then Joe asked me to give him a gift. I said I would if I could.

Do you know what he wanted? He wanted a sandcastle.
So I built a sandcastle for him.
He loved it so much that I made one just like it out of plaster of paris.
I put it in the water.
Then the little girl put Joe back in the water.
Now he swims in and out of his castle going around and around.
All of his friends come to swim with him. You've never seen so many
pretty fish.

They all swim in and out and around the little castle that I built for the fish named Joe, who was swimming in a pail the first time I saw him.

Every time I go to the beach I wonder if Joe will be there.

You can see that this gimmick can lend itself to many concepts, behavioral issues or funny stories. Actually, the children may create the most interesting stories to put in a pail.

Hat Stories

Occasionally, wearing an unusual hat will set the scene for telling a story. It will arouse interest and curiosity. Once again, the audience doesn't know what is coming next. You've got their attention which is exactly what you want. When you put on a crazy hat **you** become different. Your style changes and perhaps your voice will change too. The mood in the room will also shift. Whether you are at home, in a classroom, or presenting in front of a group, this is a sure-fire gimmick that takes very little effort and always provides entertainment.

Even in adult workshops, hats change the environment. The participants want to know, "What are you going to do? How do you use that hat?" I often ask if it sent a message when they saw it. The answer is always, "Yes!" When an idea surprises or tickles blasé adults you know that it will work with children. Try wearing:

- a wizard's pointed hat
- a tall Dr. Seuss striped hat
- a crown
- a football cheese head
- a jester's hat with bells
- an umbrella hat
- a small hat that squirts water
- a New Years Eve hat

You will find that many imaginative choices are available.

Think of a favorite story and play around with various ideas as you begin to invent your own visuals. It is a creative way to exercise your imagination.

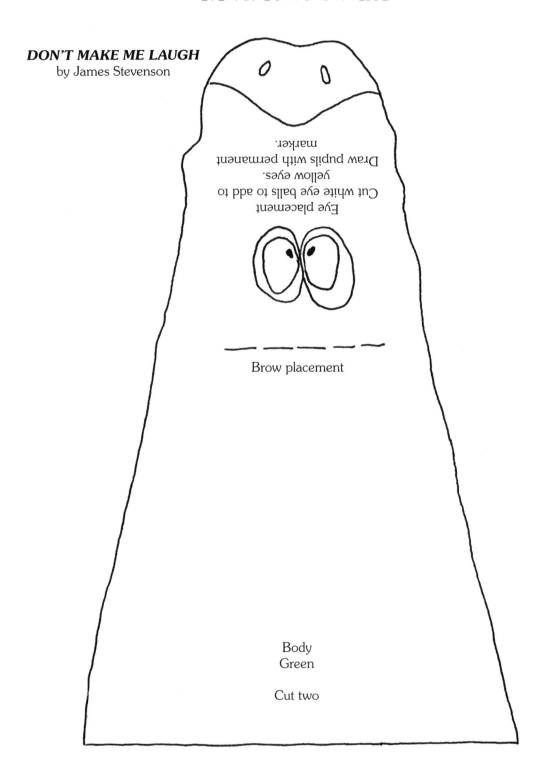

DON'T MAKE ME LAUGH
by James Stevenson

Eye placement
Cut white eye balls to add to
yellow eyes.
Draw pupils with permanent
marker.

Brow placement

Body
Green

Cut two

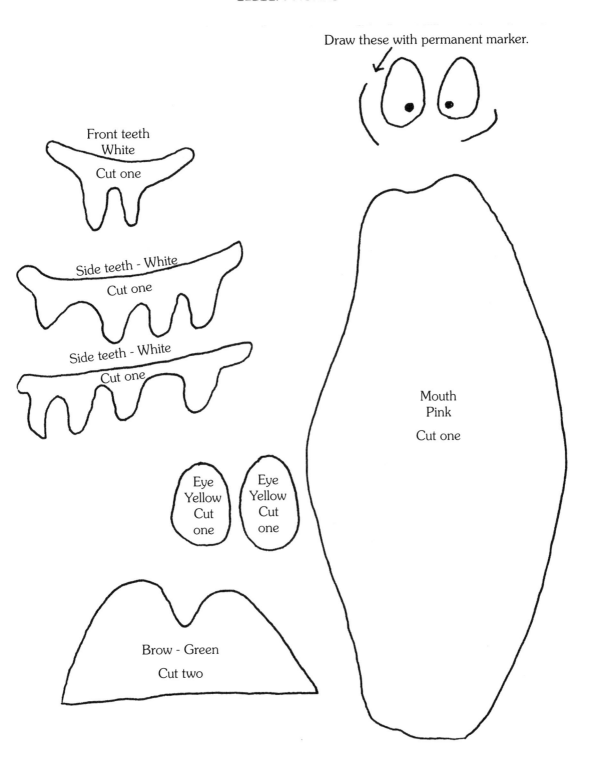

Draw these with permanent marker.

Front teeth
White
Cut one

Side teeth - White
Cut one

Side teeth - White
Cut one

Mouth
Pink
Cut one

Eye
Yellow
Cut
one

Eye
Yellow
Cut
one

Brow - Green
Cut two

Storytelling is like sailing on a thin silk thread. I'm the ferryman. My listeners make the scenery.

- Laura Simms, Storyteller

In a certain kingdom, in a certain land, in a little village, there lived...

- Russian Fairy Tales, Afanas'ev

In the High and Far-Off Times the Elephant O Best Beloved, had no trunk.

- Rudyard Kipling taken from The Elephant Child

Chapter 15
OTHER GREAT STORIES TO JUST TELL

Here Comes the Storyteller by Joe Hayes
      The Gum Chewing Rattler
      ¡Vágame, Dios!
The Hungry Thing by Jan Slepian
Jim and the Beanstalk by Raymond Briggs
Foolish Rabbit's Big Mistake by Rafe Martin
Soap! Soap! Don't Forget the Soap! retold by Tom Birdseye
There was an Old Woman by Stephen Wyllie
The Three Bears and Other Stories by Anne Rockwell
      The Three Billy Goats Gruff
      Teeny-Tiny Woman
      Lazy Jack

Crazy-Mixed-Up Stories
      How to tell familiar stories in a mixed-up fashion.

Native American Stories to explore:
      And It Is Still That Way by Byrd Baylor
      Armadillo Ray by John Beifuss
      Baby Rattlesnake told by Te Ata
      Coyote & Native American Folk Tales retold by Joe Hayes
      Coyote Stories for Children by Susan Strauss
      Coyote Tales from the Indian Pueblos by Evelyn Dahl Reed
      Doctor Coyote Native American Aesop's Fables retold by John Bierhorst
      Grandfather Stories of the Navajos from the Navajo Curriculum Center
            by Sydney Callaway
      Native American Animal Stories told by Joseph Bruchac
      The Naughty Little Rabbit and Old Man Coyote told by Estefanita Martinez
      The Wise Little Burro: Holiday Tales from Near and Far told by Joe Hayes

If your audience is old enough, you can **just tell** a story. Then you will not add visuals or unusual sounds or encourage much audience participation. It will force the listeners to really use their imaginations to picture the story in their own heads. It will also enhance their level of concentration. Even with older preschoolers, a short story told without any kind of enhancements can often be sandwiched between stories with visuals. Following are some stories that you can tell in this manner. This style is received well by children past preschool age. Being well rehearsed for these stories is a must!

Here Comes the Storyteller by Joe Hayes is a particularly good source to provide the storyteller with ideas for animated performances. I have seen him tell stories to audiences of more than one hundred children and hold them spell-bound throughout! Joe Hayes writes many of his own stories and tells them, as he might say, "Con mucho gusto!" In his book, the exciting pictures of him telling stories will certainly motivate you. He enjoys his performance as much as the kids do!

Some of his stories are tall tales. One is **The Chewing Gum Rattler** from *Here Comes the Storyteller*. Joe Hayes says this one was meant to diffuse his mother's anger at constantly finding a big wad of bubblegum in his shirt pocket. *He* says the bubblegum in his pocket saved his life one day when he met a rattlesnake. You won't believe what *he* says happened! Well, actually his mother didn't believe him either. Still, she never got mad at him again, for saving his gum in his shirt pocket.

¡ Vágame, Dios! is the perfect story for the use of bilingual skills. Joe Hayes tells it with a very intentional mix of English and Spanish. The story involves a baby chick that has fallen into the river. Because the chick fell in…a goat, a tree, a fountain, a good girl, the Queen and finally the King all get involved. Joe Hayes has contrived quite a funny ending for this tale.

In **The Hungry Thing** Jan Slepian introduces a main character who gets everything wrong. The Hungry Thing is a monster, a purple monster that charges into town wearing a sign that says FEED ME. The townspeople want to help him but they just can't understand him. He keeps saying, "Shmancakes and Ickles, shmancakes and ickles!" Finally, one of the children in town figures out what he wants. Pancakes and pickles! Soon the people shower the Hungry Thing with food, even though he does have an unusual way of saying things. When I tell this amusing story I wear a sign around my neck which says FEED ME. Often, after the story, small contests begin between pairs of kids who demand to be fed "shananas and whereal" or "grilk and trookies".

This is a challenge that soon becomes a listening/thinking game among the children.

Author, storyteller Rafe Martin says **Foolish Rabbit's Big Mistake** is a traditional Jataka tale. You will also recognize its similarity to *Chicken Little*. Little Rabbit doesn't think the sky is falling. He is sure the earth is breaking up! Of course, he scares a number of animals as he runs around predicting the earth's break up. That is, until he meets a large lion who takes a firm stand and decides to investigate the problem. There seem to be a few lessons in this story. First, don't panic and spread rumors. Second, the next time something scares you, stop and see what it is. There may be nothing to be afraid of at all. Good lessons for us all! As it turns out, what had frightened rabbit was an apple which fell from a tree under which he was sitting.

Soap! Soap! Don't Forget the Soap! is an Appalachian folk tale. Plug is a little boy who can't seem to remember much. That forgetful boy even has trouble remembering his name! Then, one bath day, his mother sends him to the store to get some soap. She is sure he will remember what to get. But just to make certain she looks in his eyes as she says, "Soap! Soap! Don't forget the soap!" On his way to the store Plug repeats her words over and over. But soon he forgets what he is supposed to remember because a big bullfrog distracts him. Along the way he repeats the angry words others say to him when he creates a problem. This causes misunderstandings with the people he meets because they think he is insulting them. Finally, he arrives at the store where a lady says, "Soap," and helps him remember what he is supposed to get. He does get home with the soap and forever after Plug remembers all of the things his mother tells him.

Jim and the Beanstalk by Raymond Briggs offers a new take on the old story of *Jack and the Beanstalk*. That huge beanstalk has grown back up to the giant's castle! It sprouts right outside

Jim's bedroom window. When Jim climbs up to the giant's castle he finds an aging giant who cannot see, has no teeth and boasts not a hair on his head. Since he has no teeth he can't eat Jim. So they talk. Jim ends up rejuvenating the giant with huge eyeglasses, false teeth and a curly red wig. The grateful giant sends Jim back down the beanstalk so that he won't be tempted to eat him. As Jim chops down the beanstalk he receives from the giant a generous surprise along with a hand-printed note.

There Was an Old Woman by Stephen Wyllie is a charming little story. The old woman had lived in her quaint little house for long years. One day a grey mouse comes to live in her thatched roof. She really doesn't mind a bit until the mouse squeaks and scratches all night long. She does not get a wink of sleep. So she gets a cat to chase the mouse away. But the cat scratches and meows and keeps her awake all night long. So she gets a dog to chase the cat away so that she may get a good night's sleep. After that, she collects even more animals. She is just trying to get a good night's sleep. All of the animals make disturbing sounds all night long. Her story is your story. You just get one problem solved when another problem pops up. This story entertains children because of the rhythm of the language and the sounds that the animals make. Adults are entertained because it is the story of the way life is.

The Three Bears and Other Stories by Anne Rockwell offers familiar fairy tales. Old fairy tales have long been a staple of the storyteller's collection. I could have listed many more but I just want to call your attention to a few with which you may be less familiar. You may have other favorites. Be sure to tell them.

The Three Billy Goats Gruff has many repetitive lines and three goats that are brothers. This is a Scandinavian tale. Children love to repeat the lines like, "Trip, Trap! Trip, Trap! Trip, Trap!" Of course, there is the troll, but he never seems too scary to young children. If he is scary, they know they are safe in their school or home. No worries. Some versions are more violent than others, so choose the version carefully. All are sure to like the Scandinavian ending which is…

"Snip, snap, snout.
        This tale's told out."

The Teeny-Tiny Woman is repetitive and cumulative. Children like the sound of the teeny-tiny woman who lives in a teeny-tiny house in a teeny-tiny village. The story goes on describing everything as teeny-tiny. Even the end will be well-received if it is told well.

Lazy Jack is the silliest boy you ever met. He doesn't think for himself. When he loses his pennies his mother tells him he should have carried them home in his pocket. So when she sends him to get milk he remembers what she said. But, carrying milk in his pocket doesn't work very well. So she gives him advice about carrying milk. He tries to use that advice when he is carrying butter. It only melts all over him. The story goes on like this until he makes a rich young girl laugh. He marries her and ends up being a gentleman. He never works a day for the rest of his life.

I wonder, was this originally social commentary about the upper class?

Crazy, Mixed-Up Stories

These are so much fun! The original 'Little Green Riding-Hood' is found in *The Read-A-Loud Handbook* by Jim Trelease. The idea is: Tell a familiar story…***all wrong!*** Make it up in a very outrageous way. Exaggerate, get the facts wrong, and change the characters. You can include new characters. The audience is sure to object! The storyteller acts very surprised and pretends to try to get it right, but keeps making mistakes. The group must know the real story so that they can begin to question your telling of it. It is all impromptu. You should probably have the first sentence in mind. But after that it takes on a life of its own. Once the children have permission to argue with you, they make the give and take very lively.

I once told a story in this fashion to a group of third graders. As the children left, a very serious boy who barely came up to my shoulders confronted me. "SO," he said with great authority, "have you ever even read that story?" He was very offended, even outraged that I would have attempted to tell a story I did not know!!! Actually, I was very pleased since it seemed to me I had totally fooled him and his friends.

Here is a sample of how I begin such a story.

ME: Little Green Riding-hood's mother wanted her to take some food to her grandmother who was ill. So Little Green Ridinghood threw a sack of potatoes over her shoulder, hopped on her motorcycle and headed for the freeway.
   (By now the audience is grumbling.)
ME: Oh, you mean, she didn't take her Grandma potatoes? No motorcycle, you say? She didn't go on the freeway? All right what did she take to Grandma? Did she drive? Okay. And you say she went through the woods? Okay, I'll start over.
   (I start over. But when she gets to the woods she meets a camel.)
KIDS: No, no she meets a wolf!
ME: Really, a wolf? Are you sure?
KIDS: Yes, yes, it's a wolf. She meets a WOLF!
ME: Okay, as she is walking in the woods she meets a shaggy grey wolf.
   (The kids begin to relax. They feel they have me straightened out now.)
ME: The wolf is very clever and chatty. He asks about her Grandma's health. Then he asks Little Red for her address and phone number which she quickly gives him.
KIDS: No, no she shouldn't, she shouldn't!
ME: No? Tell me why.
   (Go on with the story, as you choose, for as long as you choose. My story has ended in a different way each time I've told it).

Native American Stories

I live in the southwest so Native American Stories have become part of my collection of stories for children. Most of the books I have listed for you are collections of stories. I find that those in Byrd Baylor's book *And it is Still That Way* work well with preschoolers. Many of the stories in the books listed are coyote stories. Coyote is a trickster. He will make you laugh because he is trying to be so clever that sometimes he gets fooled.

Some of the Native American stories are like Aesop's fables in that they inform the listener why things are the way they are. Why does Baby Rattlesnake have fangs? Why don't dogs talk any more? Why do saguaros grow on the south side of hills? Why do dogs sniff each other's tails? Why do bears have short tails? These are stories told as they were first told perhaps thousands of years ago. They are the stories the storytellers told to help the early people make sense of their world. These are the early beginnings of the stories we tell today.

Please explore the books I have listed for stories which will best fit your audiences.

Indigenous Stories

Wherever you live you will be able to locate so-called 'native stories'. They will be valuable to the children you encounter because they often encompass their particular heritage. Explore the necessary resources to find those stories and share them with the children.

Such tales may represent stories from:
Family history and wisdom
The Appalachian Mountains
Native American tribes and Shaman stories
Ethnic cultures worldwide
Bre'r Rabbit stories
Cajun tellings
Various ancestral origins
Some of these may be told in dialect. Dialects are fun to master and offer another way to make you a distinctive storyteller.

You may find these stories among collections from:
Area museums
Town historical sites
Public libraries
Storytellers in the area

When you **just tell** stories without props or visuals, you allow the children to create the pictures for themselves. Of course, they must be mature enough to attend to your story. Then too, your descriptions and details must be colorful and clear.

Every kind of storytelling has its challenges and its gifts!

At a time when men and animals were all the
same and spoke the same language...
- traditional Navajo beginning

Joe Hayes says, that each story has a message
for the storyteller and the child. As the storyteller you
keep telling the story because you need to hear the
message over and over. Sometimes you tell a whole
story, just so you can say one important line.
- Here Comes the Storyteller by Joe Hayes

Chapter 16
CHANTS AND SONGS

The Lady with the Alligator Purse by Nadine Bernard Westcott
Lizard's Song by George Shannon
Mama Don't Allow by Thatcher Hurd
Miss Mary Mack adapted by Mary Ann Hoberman
Old Black Fly by Jim Aylesworth
Old MacDonald Had a Woodshop by Lisa Shulman
Possum Come a-Knockin' by Nancy Van Laan
Take Me Out of the Bathtub and other silly songs by Alan Katz
Today is Monday with pictures by Eric Carle
Train Leaves the Station by Eve Merriam
Whiffle Squeak by Caron Lee Cohen

There are many more. But these are the books of chants and songs I have come to know and particularly love because all can be sung or chanted with the children. While they sing, they also feel the rhythm and beat of the song. They can move with it and participate with their whole body. They can swing, sway, move their feet, and beat their hands in time to the music. They are quickly living in the middle of the experience!

Following is a brief overview of each listed selection. It should help you consider choices for your young ones.

The Lady with the Alligator Purse is a really silly song. Put into the bathtub, Timmy "ate up all the soap. So mama called the doctor. In came the doctor, in came the nurse and in came the Lady with the Alligator Purse." When asked for a diagnosis and to name a remedy, the Lady with the Alligator Purse prescribed…PIZZA! I said this was a silly song. Children find it hilarious!

Lizard's Song is about his song, and about Bear who wants to take it. Somehow Bear could not sing Lizard's song. He just couldn't remember it. In the end he sings his *own* song. Shouldn't we all do that? This song and book have a satisfying ending, encouraging us all to be ourselves. The words and music are printed in the book.

Mama Don't Allow is a song. It was once done in a spirited arrangement in the big band era. The book includes a musical arrangement of this old traditional song. It lends itself to creating your own new chorus. And, as author Thatcher Hurd says, "Play it **loud!**"

Miss Mary Mack is called a hand-clapping rhyme. It works well to establish a cadence and rhythm. I seem to remember that I also jumped rope to it as a child. It certainly can be chanted just for fun.

I first heard **Old Black Fly** sung at a CDA (Child Development Associate) music workshop. The leader, Sue Kujawski, said that when she read stories she often heard them as songs. In her head she heard "Josuha 'Fit the Battle of Jericho'" when she read *Old Black Fly*. She also claimed that once you *sing* a story the children will never let you just *read* or *tell* it again. I think she's right!

When you try it, you will find that the words of this particular rhyming story fit very well with the music she suggested.

Old MacDonald Had a Woodshop is clever. MacDonald has a woodshop full of tools that make great noises like *zztt, zztt*. That's the saw's sound. The hammer goes tap, tap. This cute song is easily sung to *Old MacDonald Had a Farm*. It is sure to be a favorite of the girls because Old MacDonald is a W-O-M-A-N! Of course, the boys will like it because of all the tools and the loud noises they make. This song and book may well become a classic!

Possum Come a-Knockin' may be a song you remember from your childhood. The repetitive words are delightful. "Possum come a-knockin' at the door, at the wee small door." It is written in dialect and is charming. It has been used as a jump rope chant too.

Take Me Out of the Bathtub uses the tune and phrasing of *Take Me Out to the Ballgame*. "Take me out of the bathtub. Take me out of the suds. I've been here soaking since half past two. I feel so sudsy and wrinkle-y too." You know just how this little kid feels as he begs to get to dry land. The kids are sure to love it!

"Today is Monday, today is Monday. Monday, string beans, Tuesday, spaghetti, Wednesday, ZOOOOP. All you hungry children, come and eat it up!" You and the children will journey through the week with a variety of yummy foods. You may even insert some of your own choices into this silly song.

Train Leaves the Station offers rhyme, rhythm and repetition. "Snake in the grass, angel in heaven, train leaves the station at seven-o-seven." Each number has its own rhyme, so you can get from one to nine with a number of fine lines. Then, repeat it all over again if you want to. "Nonsense," you say. And I say, "You're right!"

Whiffle Squeak is a story in rhyme. If it sounds familiar, you may know it as *'Aiken Drum' Who Lived on the Moon*. It was commonly known as early as 1821. This story's language is especially colorful. Its characters all live in the sea and have ingenious names like Gazook Gaboot, a monster who ate jellyfish squish. The words fill your mouth like an elegant caramel.

I have chosen not to list the nursery rhyme and popular finger play songs that have been made into picture books. Many are available and they, too, would make interesting additions to your storytelling collection.

The previous songs and chants are valuable to your story collection because you will be able to use them to tame an audience. When you need to stretch until the rest of a group arrives, these can be quite helpful. I also include them when my audience is not settling down or needs a change of pace to allow the performance to continue. My own children will be happy to tell you that I do not sing well. But, I do these kinds of songs with groups of kids because they are such fun that the quality of the music is not an issue. Enjoy!

Chapter 17
MAKING UP YOUR OWN STORIES

"To invent is to come alive." Vivian Paley

Children tell stories all the time. They will happily relate how they fell down or what Grandpa bought for them at the store. They may tell you what they did over the weekend or about their dog having babies. It may be difficult to tell the real stories from those they have imagined. So they can invent stories. Actually writing stories may require your help. The following ideas may be of some assistance.

Inventing stories with children

As story starters, begin your questions with these words:

Who?
What?
When?
Where
Why?
How?

Children will often answer questions with "I dunno [sic]." Probe further by asking the same question in a different way.

For example:

- Who do you think could have painted this stop sign green? Take a guess.
- What happened here or what is happening here? Pretend this was happening to you.
- When do you think this could have started? Who could have been there?
- Where is he going? If you were him where would you be going?
- Why is she smiling? What makes you smile? What could have made her smile?
- How does he feel? How would you feel? How do you think you would feel?

Note: After I write such questions I try to answer them myself. If I cannot, I rephrase the question or discard it.

If they are reluctant to answer, you might tell them that you are sure they have an answer in their mind and encourage them to think about it. Sometimes you can wait for the answer, but do not embarrass them by waiting too long. Perhaps they need an example of what *your answer* would be. Praise the children who come up with their own answers. Discourage repeating an answer already given. However, if a very shy child does participate by giving someone else's answer, I would accept it and thank her for participating. Another time she may be more comfortable and share her own answer. As you begin this style of questioning you may find children reluctant to participate. Show your interest in their response. As they find that you do not have a 'right' response in mind, and are willing to accept creative answers, they will begin to share their thoughts.

A story *will* develop when you ask open-ended questions or those with many possible answers. An open-ended question is one that cannot be answered with yes or no or single 'right, one word' answers.

Do not have great expectations. Many young children are not yet aware of the beginning, middle, and end of stories. Vivian Paley (see Adult Resources), in her books about writing with young children, suggests that beginning stories may be just one word. Her example was "Mother". A one word story said it all for an almost two-year-old and the other kids acted it out by showing what Mother did. She fixed her hair, vacuumed the rug, washed dishes, rocked the baby, etc. As children mature, vocabulary increases. The organization and stories will come too. This is true especially if someone has nurtured them with the experience of telling stories.

The following are ideas for jump-starting storie:
- Keep a file of crazy pictures, some of which are real, and some that are unique, staged photos. Then, ask the open-ended questions above. This can be an individual or a group activity.
- Keep in a corner of the room a story starter box that might include hats, capes, costumes, dresses, jackets, props, stuffed animals, and puppets. Children will soon be acting out some scenario that they have envisioned. If you think about it, dramatic play is really a form of storytelling.
- The *Storytelling Stone* is a story that fascinates me. In his book, *Awakening the Hidden Storyteller*, Robin Moore retells the tale of the storytelling stone. This is a Seneca Indian legend of how storytelling began. In prehistory, a small boy finds the stone in a clearing in the forest. The stone offers to tell him a story in exchange for a few birds he has caught. The boy agrees. In the next four days the stone reveals much about the world to the boy and his whole family. Each time the stone tells a story it receives a gift of a bird, berries, fish or corn. Once the gift is given, the story can be told. On the fourth day the stone announces that it will tell no more stories. The boy and his sister are sad until the stone explains that now they are the storytellers. To keep the stories alive *they* must tell the stories to others. Read the version of the story as told by Robin Moore. It is quite lyrical! The preceding may serve as a another great story-starter. Once the children have heard the original story, ask them a question. "What is *our* story going to be about today?" Encourage them to suggest the who, what, when, where, why and how of their story. As they repeatedly make up stories, quality will improve. Children under the age of four and a half or five may not understand the concept of answering who, what, when, where, why and how questions related to story writing. Older children will relish the opportunity to explain their world via a story. Stories may end up sounding like Aesop's Fables or the idea may merely encourage stories of everyday life. You might also get some pretty wild fantasies. It's worth a try!
- Consider the use of some form of instant story-starters. You can decorate a box or can containing slips of paper to be drawn out one at a time by a child. These slips state story beginnings. For example, a small dog was running down a sidewalk when a cat stepped in his way. The cat had beautiful long white hair and lavender eyes. She told the dog that she was a magic cat. What happened next? The entire group may contribute ideas or the child who drew the slip may tell the story.

Let your imagination run wild as you create enticing scenarios. Keep adding slips to your container so that new stories will be born. Another variation would be to have separate containers, one holding possible characters, another with places where the story might happen, and a third with events that could happen, jokes, or unforeseen happenings. Making up these kinds of stories could be an activity that happens whenever you have extra time. The adult, of course, becomes the writer unless the children are old enough to do it themselves. Be sure to share these stories with their parents.

The result of experiences like these is often that by age four or five children can successfully offer more of a real story. Often they still produce rather disconnected stories or series of unrelated events. This may reflect the level of organization going on in the brain. Because some kids seem so smart these days we forget that they're still sorting things out in their world. Child development proceeds at a steady pace. We can stuff them with information and experience but young bodies and minds will still march to the beat of the developmental drummer. Just as we all scribble before we draw or write we will first tell or write incomplete stories. These small stories are the beginning of a valuable process.

When you invent and write down stories with children, you help them become aware of the following:

Words are made up of letters.
Words have meaning.
Words can be put down on paper to be read.
Words represent ideas, things, people or animal characters, feelings and events.
Words can be arranged to explain ideas, describe feelings, and tell stories.
These are all important concepts needed when learning the art of reading.

Consider and use pictures and illustrations wisely. When learning to read, one also looks at and reads pictures. Often, a picture represents what is happening in the story. In a good picture book children read the pictures. The illustrations give readers and listeners clues as to what the story is about. When choosing picture books, look for illustrations on the same page as the related text. Look for artistic, realistic or humorous drawings and those which help the child understand the story.

Adults Inventing Stories

These are ideas that can stimulate stories:
- *Use a very large key to stimulate answers to:*
  What kind of a door does it open? Where?
  Who was there? What happened then?
- *Consider a tiny, tiny hippopotamus whose story is yet to be told.*
  How did he get to be this small?
  Who found this hippo?
  What will happen now?
- *Begin with an antique. Though it does not have an obvious use it may well suggest a tale.*
- *Weave a series of riddles through a storyline.*
- *Display some object obviously painted many times. Ask:*
  Who painted you this color? Why?

Who owned you next? Why did they paint you?

• *Use a simple drawing to begin. A figure like Harold and his purple crayon may lead to a new story of his adventures.*

Where is he going today?

What will he do there?

• *An elementary piece of magic holds potential. Does it connect to any character to be imagined?*

Who did this magic trick?

What occurred when she did it?

(i.e. *Old Woman and Her Animals* in Chapter 10, String Stories.)

• *Make a string figure which develops in a fascinating way.* Stories to go with these are further from reality and are merely a diversion for the audience while you manipulate the string.

• *Create cut or torn paper figures. Take an image central to the story and recreate it in paper form while you are telling the story.*

• *Tell a crazy or mixed-up version of a story familiar to the audience.* Allow them the freedom to argue with you and correct your version of the tale. This is loads of fun for all involved.

• *Find an unusual noisemaker to weave into a great story.* I have a dog toy that squeaks. I use it when I tell *The Squeaky Old Bed*, a folktale from Puerto Rico. I also have a cylinder that makes the sound of thunder. I know it will weave itself into a story soon. A collection of small musical instruments will certainly merit a story.

• *Re-write existing books with your audience.* This will be a valuable experience for children and a good way to create a new story. Many authors have used the idea to produce an original story. For example: *The Three Little Wolves and the Big Bad Pig or The Fourth Little Pig.* It is exceptionally easy to rewrite Margaret Wise Brown's *The Important Book.* Jeff Brown's book titled *Flat Stanley* is fun to enhance with your own photos of Flat Stanley's adventures in your own home and community.

• *Write a well-known tale from the viewpoint of one of the characters.* What would the Goldilocks story sound like from the viewpoint of Baby Bear?

• *Substitute themes.* A book like *I Went Walking, What Did You See?* might become *I Went to the Zoo. What Did You See?* Other ideas could include:

Look in the fridge. What do you see?

I heard a duck. What did it say?

• *Use pattern books like Brown Bear, Brown Bear What Do You See?* Substitute a word or phrase and keep the same pattern. *Big Mac* uses this device.

• *My Magic Pail* holds a story. Create a small story. Cut a piece of adding machine tape on which you will write the story. Add pictures if you like. When finished, roll up the tape and tuck it into the pail. Bring out the pail. Suggest that there is a story in the pail that you would like to tell. Pull out the roll of paper. Begin to unroll it as you start the story. I don't know whether this is an original idea or if I have adapted it from something I've read somewhere. My magic pail is about three inches tall. Choose any size you like.

Think about using your magic pail in the classroom, to introduce the concept of the day or week. Tailor your story to deal with a classroom problem or allow your story to deal with an emotion or a fantasy. Perhaps, on a given day your magic pail will tell a joke or raise a question to be discussed by the group. Remember to make it a bit of magic as you present the story. The first story will be a surprise. Then, when you show the pail another day, they may expect the same story...again. There is always the chance that there will be a different story there by now. This gimmick holds the same charm as the hold on your lap stories since it is a kind of surprise.

• *Make books.* For inspiration explore *Making Books That Fly, Fold, Wrap, Hide, Pop Up, Twist, and Turn* by Gwen Diehn. This is a book full of books. It is comprised of many exciting book making ideas. In addition, it includes some of the history of books.

Personal Experiences with Story Writing

In *Creative Storytelling* author Jack McGuire suggests that writing a story involves asking the question 'What if?' So, identify a character that will inhabit your story and ask it, "What do you do now? Who is with you? Or whom do you meet? Where are you? What is it like there? What happened to you? How did that come to be?" Your characters know the answers. Just check with them and the tale will tell itself.

While it may be difficult to create truly exciting story, try it anyway! It's a good exercise in creativity. Often, your story improves after a few tellings. Always listen to off-hand comments the kids make or unexpected things that happen while you tell a story. In a workshop the other day, I was telling an old story. I was about to say, "When the wolf got there..." Just at that moment a cell phone rang. Everyone heard it. So I continued with, "When the wolf got there... the cell phone rang." Everyone laughed and we continued the story. Eventually that may become part of my telling of that story.

Creating Drawn Stories

These are usually simple stories with unsophisticated drawings. People of all ages are attracted to such stories and are often surprised that you've drawn something recognizable. Inspiration for these can be found in Richard Thompson books, *Draw & Tell* and *Frog's Riddle*. My personal favorite is *The Ghost on Pedersen's Farm*.

Snagging Characters

You might snag a good character from one of your other stories and tell a different story about him. Here is what I did. In a torn-paper story from *Mudluscious* called *Lost, Left and All Gone* I took the character, Mojo who lived in a jungle and wove him into a drawing which turned out to be a lion. This lion ran right off the drawing board when Mojo yelled, "GO AWAY!" I found the lion drawing in Sid Hoff's book *Drawing Letters and Numbers.* See Chapter 8 for the drawing and the story.

Utilizing Round-Robin Stories with Puppets

This idea works with a small group and a participating audience or, in my case, three children and a grandma!

It was after Christmas, I was tired as we'd been up all night because one of the twins had had a bad nosebleed and swallowed so much blood that she got very sick. I had been awakened by her mom screaming for me to come help her. When we saw the pale blue and white bathroom heavily splattered with blood, we both panicked. It looked as if someone had been killed in there. As her mom and I looked at little Madeline we were afraid she was seriously ill. The emergency room seemed the best solution, so off went Mom, Dad and a pale little Madeline Ann. Grandpa, Maxine, Cassidy and I waited for four hours to hear that she was fine. The blood from the nosebleed which settled in her stomach, had been rejected all over my bathroom. We all fell into bed for a few hours of sleep before they headed for the airport. Soon enough, we were all up dressing. After our good-byes, Grandpa took them to the airport, returned home, and fell asleep in the family room. We were both exhausted.

That's when the phone rang.

Daddy and the three kids requested a ride back to our house. They had had ticket problems. Mom opted for a flight home with the puppy and they were all scheduled on a much later flight. So, Grandpa went back to the airport.

Soon, a very exhausted Daddy and Grandpa dragged through the front door. Even the three kids were limp. I volunteered to take them to a bedroom and tell them stories to settle them down for a nice nap. Daddy and Grandpa had a football game to watch. Can you guess what happened? Yes, Grandpa and Daddy fell peacefully asleep as the game droned on. Meanwhile, in the bedroom the kids were reviving. Any thought I had of a nap was gone. I told stories until I ran out of them.

The children still had to be quiet because Grandpa and Daddy were napping. Puppets were the solution. There was a large basket, overflowing with them, right in the room. Each child chose a puppet. We then began a round-robin story wherein characters, in turn, told part of the story then stopped and asked the next puppet to tell what happened after that. It went on and on. I wish I had recorded it. The story was convoluted, silly, sometimes dull and suddenly funny and exciting. It went on for an hour and a half with new puppets subbing for tired ones, calls for drinks, snacks and obviously no thought of naps. Then, suddenly, it was airport time again. Goodbye hugs and kisses were given all around. What a special time!

Again, that's how an idea was born or at least acted out... out of necessity. A much shorter story could be told in small groups or a small group might do it for an audience (the rest of the class). The quality of the stories won't always be high but some interesting ideas will emerge and the children will begin to realize that everyone can tell stories. The puppets add the quality of separation or protection, freeing some more reserved children to participate. The really shy child may just make the sound of the animal, "Peep, peep" and the rest of the group can guess what that really means. Do experiment. Beware! After this activity the puppets in the book corner may begin storytelling all by themselves.

Use an Unusual Purchase to Trigger a Story

One day last summer I found three small bears on sale. They were dressed in Halloween costumes Here was a story begging to be told. Guess what happened when I asked the bears why they were wearing costumes? They told the story of how they met the three blind mice.

This story is similar to the original *Goldilocks and the Three Bears* except that Hansel, Gretel, and Cinderella are dressed as the three blind mice. It takes place on Halloween Night. While the bears are out trick-or-treating, Hansel, Gretel and Cinderella come to their house begging for candy. After eating the bears' dinner stew they decide to stay around to say, "Thank you!" They don't break any furniture. They ask Mama Bear for her recipes after enjoying her dinner. They cut Baby

Bear a string of orange pumpkins to play with and Papa Bear declares them much better guests than that silly Goldilocks who broke things, got scared, and ran away. As they leave, Mama Bear invites them to come back to play any time. Hansel, Gretel and Cinderella depart with full tummies after making some new friends in the woods. That's why this story is called: *The Three Bears Meet the Three Blind Mice (well sort of).*

Currently there are few Halloween stories acceptable in schools. Ghosts and witches are not always considered appropriate. The value of a positive story is that you can tell it and truly say, "Happy Halloween".

In *Soul Between the Lines*, Dorothy Randall Gray says, "Inside of you lives a powerful spirit. It is something you are born with, something you use every day without even thinking. I want you to know that within this spirit is a treasure chest of unlimited creative power." She continues, "Think of writing as the key that unlocks the chest. And as you open this chest, your spirit will bless you with greater awareness, self-discovery, and transformation." May it be so for you!

The possibilities of what **could** have happened to characters of familiar stories are endless. Again, I encourage you to begin to write some of your own stories.

As we let our own light shine, we unconsciously give other people permission to do the same.

- Nelson Mandela, 1994 Inaugural Speech

Chapter 18
DEVELOPING A STORYTELLING WORKSHOP
Adult Storytelling Workshops

- Handouts…what and why?
- What to take to a workshop
- Format for workshop
- Evaluation Form
- Certificate of Attendance
- Your own storyteller card
- Presenting to preschool or public school classes
- What to take to a storytelling session

At a certain point as a storyteller, you will find yourself bubbling over with new ideas and stories. As your reputation for storytelling grows, you may be asked to present a workshop. This chapter includes specific plans for such events. You will, of course, tailor your plan to suit your own requirements. Consider the importance of:

- providing a storytelling handout, list, patterns, directions
- telling many stories with visuals
- including a "Make-and-Take It" session
- selecting materials
- planning a successful experience for the group of adults or children

Let us begin!

Handouts…what and why?

Develop a basic handout as the skeleton of what you will discuss during your workshop. Briefly state your ideas about storytelling and list the titles of stories you have found to be successful. This gives your audience valuable information to refer to in the future.

As a beginning storyteller, it is difficult to know which stories to tell. Lists of stories provide amateurs a place to start. A storyteller should own as many of the books he/she uses as possible. It is important to support authors. It is important to be able to show these books. Since many people are very visual, seeing a book means being more likely to remember it. At a minimum you must own your favorites! Such books are a *storyteller's toys*. I treasure my books. I hope you do too! Encourage those in your workshops to do likewise!

As you present storytelling workshops you will invent your own style. I choose to speak very casually and without a prepared script. However, I must be aware of the points I intend to make. My handout serves as my map to travel through a four-hour workshop. Given a handout, listeners really do not need to take many notes. This means they can concentrate on things I show them, books I hold up, or visuals I present. No time is wasted with spelling authors' names or repeating book titles because all are clearly listed on the handout. I want my audience listening and concentrating, not writing.

Because I know I will never have all of the answers for the questions participants ask, I don't worry about that. I am familiar with many books and stories, but not all stories, book titles or authors. The audience is always pleased to be able to give me a new title or a new tale. I welcome their input. I am there to give them the benefit of my experience. They will not always agree with my answers or beliefs. Luckily, there is plenty of room for variety of attitude and style in storytelling.

What to take to a workshop

Basic needs:
- a table easel to hold the white board
- white board pens and an eraser
- a felt cover for your white board (Now it is a felt board.)
- scissors for each participant
- white glue
- possibly needles, thread, a few pincushions
- books you recommend
  (Take lots of these and be sure to put your name in them.)
- copies of stories to accompany visuals and original stories
- handouts, instructions, patterns and a list of ideas for stories and visuals
- visuals to represent a variety of storytelling possibilities
- individually bagged kits for stories to be made that day
- visuals and a list of the stories you plan to tell (for your use)
- your plan for the workshop (your handout with special personal notes)
- CD player and children's CD's to play as class enters
- a bottle of drinking water
- your storyteller business cards

Format for a workshop

These are the things you might do:
- Wear a crazy hat to greet people as they enter.
- Play children's music to set the mood as participants enter.
- Introduce yourself and give a thumbnail sketch of the workshop.
- Begin by having the participants tell stories to each other. Have them pair off and take turns. Suggest that they tell personal stories related to their children or family. Funny stories are good. All stories must be short. Some stories may be shared with the group, if time allows. Having them each tell a story reinforces the concept that they are **already** storytellers.
- Distribute the storytelling handout. Go through this handout of storytelling philosophy and resource lists. Keep this brief but be sure to highlight important points.
- If participants will be making particular visuals, tell them the accompanying stories.
- Distribute a packet of other handouts including patterns and. sketches of drawn stories.
- Pass out individual kits and give final verbal instructions.
- Let them get started!
- In twenty minutes begin a 'show and tell' of other visuals you have brought and tell more stories.

- Participants are encouraged to continue to work on their visuals while the stories are being told. Tell three or four stories and then stop. They will continue to make their visuals.
- After twenty or thirty minutes tell them more of your other stories with visuals. Call attention to the list of ideas. (Chapter headings of this book give you an idea of how you might list a variety of visuals.)

The ideal workshop is four hours long. The average number of participants ranges from twenty-five to forty–five and could certainly be fewer. If you're doing a workshop for more than forty-five, consider bringing an assistant with you to help answer craft questions, distribute kits and glue bottles, etc. Some groups who sponsor workshops will offer you a volunteer assistant.

A four-hour workshop allows the presenter to share numerous stories, present philosophy and introduce many new books to the audience. The advantage to participants is that they will finish their visuals, get excited about their ability to be storytellers, and go home ready to use their own creativity.

"Make-and-Take It Workshops" are a terrific way to encourage people to begin their own storytelling journey. If they make a little set of keys to help them tell *Goodnight Gorilla* they may just **tell that story to some children**. My props don't usually take a lot of time to make. Typically four or five visuals can be made in a workshop.

Keep a list of materials needed for "Make-and-Take It" stories done in workshops. Note sizes of felt pieces (where appropriate) and how many pieces to a yard of fabric. Keep track of colors and sizes needed for each story. This saves much time. When I am really organized I also keep track of how much of any given material I have left over. Frequently you purchase more than needed due to packing (i.e., 25 in a package and you only need 10). Note this: I also list my sources since it is easy to forget where I finally found something like 'little yellow plastic bananas'!

After philosophy, storytelling, and visual-making, the morning session concludes. After lunch, participants eagerly complete their visuals. Continue to tell stories and show ideas, picture books and adult storytelling resources. At this time I also present ideas for writing stories with children. Even very young children are capable of contributing to a story written by their group.

You will experience the nicest audiences at storytelling workshops. There are always two or three good souls who will stay to help you pack up. Invest in a small, wheeled, luggage carrier. You can stack two big plastic boxes on top of each other, place them on the carrier and secure them with bungee cords. This will save time and your back as you transport materials.

Evaluation Form

You may enjoy handing out a small evaluation sheet at the end of your session. At the end of this chapter, I have included one I often use. The advantage of getting this feedback is that you can improve your next workshop. It is also a boost for your ego since your audience is usually full of positive responses. You will find that teachers never get enough handouts. Although I usually provide thirty or more pages, some people will still ask for MORE!

Certificate of Attendance

You might also consider making up a certificate of attendance. This is often provided by the organization sponsoring the workshop. In case it is not, it is nice to have one available. Most schools, preschools and day care centers keep such signed certificates on file for each teacher since state laws often demand a certain number of extra hours of training per year. Again, I've included one I use at the end of this chapter.

Your own storyteller card

Consider designing a storyteller business card for yourself. My card is a composite of my ideas and professional help from my daughter, Robin, and another artist. Both sides of the 4x6 card were used. Only general information is included. Fees are not listed. You may charge differently for "Make-and-Take It Workshops", idea workshops, storytelling sessions with children and general talks for teachers. Talk to the people who may be interested in having you present to determine your fee. Try to find out what sort of an event they are interested in and who will be present. Is this audience children or adults? If children are involved, how old are they and how many groups are there? Think about how much prep work will be needed to make kits. Ask how many people will be attending. You can always call them back to discuss your fee after you have considered all those aspects.

Presenting to preschool or public school classes

When presenting to preschool or public school classes, ask for a schedule of times, ages and numbers of children expected. You might ask the office or the organizing teacher for this information ahead of time since staff are always pressed for time.

You need to:
- Take a basket of stories you expect to tell.
- Know how many sessions you will be expected to do.
- Determine time allotted for each group.
- Make enough expendable items to cover each group. (A torn paper story like *Red Woolen Blanket* needs a fresh sheet of paper for each group.)
- Since you have timed each story, you will be able to adjust to a group who can stay ten more minutes or one who must leave in 3-5 minutes.
- Remain flexible with possible time adjustments in mind. (Consult the teachers about how long their groups can stay.)
- Expect the teacher *to be less than engaged.* **But do expect the teacher to stay.** *You do not know this group*, individual children, their habits, or rules about leaving the room or what to do if a child is acting out. Utilize the teacher as needed.
- Plan at least one active story or activity to be used if the kids are restless.
    Ideas for activities include:
        We're going to the zoo, zoo, zoo.
        Do you want to go too, too, too?
        Oh, I see a kangaroo.
        Let's all be kangaroos!
        (Hop around the room for a brief time)

        We're going to the zoo, zoo, zoo.
        Do you want to go too, too, too?
        Oh, I see an elephant.
        Let's all be elephants!

(Clasp your hands and let them hang down and swing them like a trunk while you walk around like elephants.)

Become many other animals for as long as you need to work out the wiggles. Be sure to be prepared to quiet them down with a car trip. Here they must pretend to get in the car, fasten their seat belts, and simmer down so as not to distract the driver. Or you might sing a movement song with them. Participation stories work well and keep the group in one place.

Just as I always tell children the titles and authors of the books I read to them, I also try to mention who wrote the story I will tell. Sometimes you will simply say, "This is a story that someone made up a long time ago to tell to their children."

What to take to a storytelling session
- table easel or regular easel to hold up the white board
- white board, pens and an eraser
- felt cover for white board (Now it is a felt board.)
- a bottle of water (You may be far from a drinking fountain…in Arizona that's important!)
- more stories than you think you will need (You cannot tell what will happen!)
- any special objects
- very detailed directions to the school and a phone number in case you get lost!!!

Preparing adults for storytelling is extremely exciting and rewarding and yet, I always feel so appreciated when I am telling stories, especially to children.

Whatever you are doing with stories, enjoy yourself!

CERTIFICATE OF ATTENDANCE

_____

Name of Participant

Attended a Four-Hour Workshop entitled:
"STORYTELLING WITH YOUNG CHILDREN"
Subjects included:
Ways to make stories visible to the young child,
Picture Books, Storytelling Resources
and
"Make-And-Take" Session

_____   _____

Date   Signature of Instructor, Eileen Hoard

EVALUATION FORM
Eileen Hoard, Storyteller

The most valuable parts of the workshop to me were: (circle one or more)

New Ideas   Make-and-Take It   Handouts

General Information   Hearing Stories   The Books

Motivation to do my own storytelling

Rate the overall quality of the presentation. (1 is low, 10 is high)

    1   2   3   4   5   6   7   8   9   10

Was this presentation a valuable use of your time? (1 is low, 10 is high)

    1   2   3   4   5   6   7   8   9   10

I could have used more _____ .

I could have used less _____ .

One Idea I'm going to use is _____ .

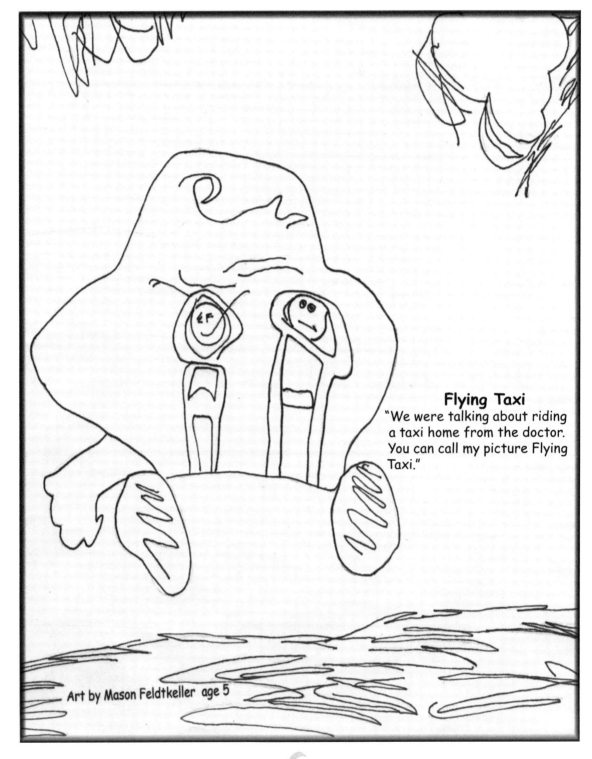

Flying Taxi
"We were talking about riding a taxi home from the doctor. You can call my picture Flying Taxi."

Art by Mason Feldtkeller age 5

Chapter 19
BITS AND PIECES...
Some last thoughts

- Stories and visuals "in waiting"
- Storing stories
- List of useful materials...some basics for making visuals
- Drawing Board, Felt Board and Carrier
- A Carpenter's Nail Apron/Storyteller's Apron
- Unusual resources for storytelling visuals

Stories and visuals "in-waiting"

I always have some stories I'm thinking about...maybe for a couple of years...until the idea suddenly comes to me of how to best enhance this particular story. If you have a computer you could keep a running list of stories "in-waiting" or you might keep a Storytelling Notebook with a section for stories you might do someday.

Sometimes I have visuals for which I haven't found a story. For example currently I have:
- petroglyph stickers from the Art Museum which might form the basis of a drawn story,
- a colorful, noisy, group of small musical instruments which might be played by *The Bremen Town Musicians*,
- a pointed, pink, princess hat with a veil,
- a yellow, satin hat, and
- a funny mask with a large red nose and a bushy mustache.

Storing stories

If you are just beginning as a storyteller you may not see the need to be concerned with organizing or labeling stories. When you only have five or ten stories it's not very important, but as the numbers grow it becomes helpful to be able to *find* the story you seek!

Use large recloseable plastic bags labeled with story name, author, and timing.

In the bag:

1. Include a colorful paperback copy of the book. Make a typed or computer copy of the text of the story since this is much easier to refer to when learning the story. It also saves time looking for the book which you may have mislaid or loaned to someone.
2. Note how long it takes you to tell the story. That will be helpful when putting together a storytelling session. You may also need to be aware of timing when a group unexpectedly mentions that they must leave in five minutes. Of course, you won't start a ten minute story if you only have five minutes.

3. Add any notes you have made to help you learn the story.
4. Insert any appropriately sized visuals and props.

List of useful materials...some basics for making visuals

Colored pipe cleaners in wonderful true colors
Felt...buy by the yard for bigger pieces or 9"x 12" sheets in good true colors
 (Purchase a bright red if you are identifying it as red to young children).
Cotton batting
Small plastic miniatures and toys
String...colors and off-white for string stories
Construction paper
Tissue paper for "showers" of butterflies, hearts etc.
Wooden spoons
Acrylic paints and paint brushes
Various buttons
Small metal candy tins
Scraps of colorful yarns of different weights
Small rigid paper plates
Tongue depressors for handles on paddle stories
Empty pizza boxes
Shoe boxes
1-1/4" wood blocks
A large cape
An old, black man's hat
Other dress-ups and costumes
Large recloseable plastic bags for storing stories
Plastic sandwich bags for making individual kits for make-and-take sessions
Tacky glue for various uses
Modge Podge for decoupage (available in craft stores)
Erasable dry markers for drawn stories
White board eraser

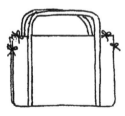

Drawing Board, Felt Board and Carrier

As a traveling storyteller I go to public schools, preschools and workshops. I never know how far I will have to walk from the parking lot or whether I will need to move from room to room. My big white board can be a problem to carry. The carrier is my solution. The carrier is made to sling over my shoulder. This leaves my arms and hands free to carry my basket of stories, etc.

When planning the sequence of stories for a presentation always choose to tell felt board stories before drawn stories. This allows you to just pull off the felt cover and be ready to draw! Audiences do not particularly like to wait while the storyteller puts the felt cover on and adjusts it. Keeping the flow of the session is important. Avoid any unnecessary pauses. Audience attention is key.

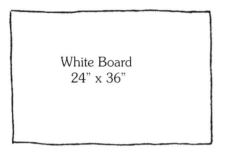

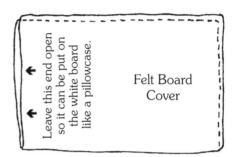

Materials for White Board, Felt Board and Carrier:

One white board, 24"x 36" Purchase a large framed white board at an office supply or go to a lumber yard and have one cut. You may have to buy a 4'x 8' sheet of white board and have it cut into the 24"x 36" board. Have the remainder cut into smaller boards. These make great gifts for adults or kids. Add a few white board pens to complete the gift.

Light blue felt 73"x 25" will become the felt board cover. Fold it in half and sew it together on two sides using 1/4" seams. Blue will be the most compatible background for most of the felt stories you may make.

The carrier is made from sturdy upholstery fabric. It works well if the upholstery material is just a bit stiff. The finished carrier should be 74" x 26". Turn the edges of the fabric under to keep it from fraying. A dark color of fabric will be the most serviceable. Buy enough fabric so that you can turn edges under 1/2" and sew them down. Add a few inches to the finished dimension given. Heavy fabric can be bulky to turn under, so turn it under with your hand before having it cut to insure that you are buying enough yardage.

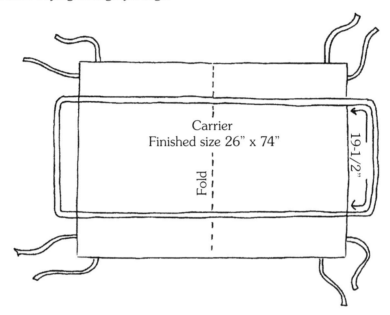

Carrier
Finished size 26" x 74"

Fold

19-1/2"

Carrier handles are most easily made from a strong, dark braid or flat cording. Seven yards of cording should give you enough to make the straps longer if needed and cut eight 7" ties for the sides. (I am 5'2" and my strap is 19-1/2" on each side.) Measure your carrier and handles to see whether seven yards of cording will be enough.

**A Carpenter's Nail Apron/
Storyteller's Apron**
These aprons are inexpensive.
Typically they are made of
lightweight canvas. You can put
your hand into its three man-sized

pockets. Often they have advertisements printed on them. Cover those ads by adding bright fabric or felt shapes to the outside of the pocket using Tacky Glue or Wonder Under. Tied around your waist this apron is a convenient place for you to hide: white board pens, string story cords, folded paper fans for cut paper stories, small scissors and felt board pieces. The apron will save you from searching the bottom of your basket for those little items and will assist your presentation's flow.

Unusual resources for storytelling visuals

The Fairy Tale Doll Company
P.O. Box 572433
Tarzana, CA 91357-2433
Call Stephenee at: (310) 415-2817

www.thefairytaledollcompany.com

Fairy Tale Dolls are reversible dolls and have other characters hidden under the main character's skirt. For example, when you turn the Goldilocks doll over you will find The Three Bears hiding there. The whole story is available in one doll.

Oriental Trading Company Inc.
Omaha, NE 68103-2308

They have all sorts of inexpensive items available. They carry unusual hats, small plastic animals and themed party décor. Ask for a free catalog.

Schrock's International
110 Water Street
P. O. Box 538
Bolivar, OH 44612

This company carries many types of wood blocks and figures. This is my resource for 1-1/4" blocks for *Fly's Castle*. It also carries ribbons, beads and other craft materials. Send for a free catalog.

> *As we live we are transmitters*
> *of life. When we fail to transmit life*
> *life fails to flow through us.*
> *- A poem by poet, D.H.Lawrence*
> *Titled We Are Transmitters*

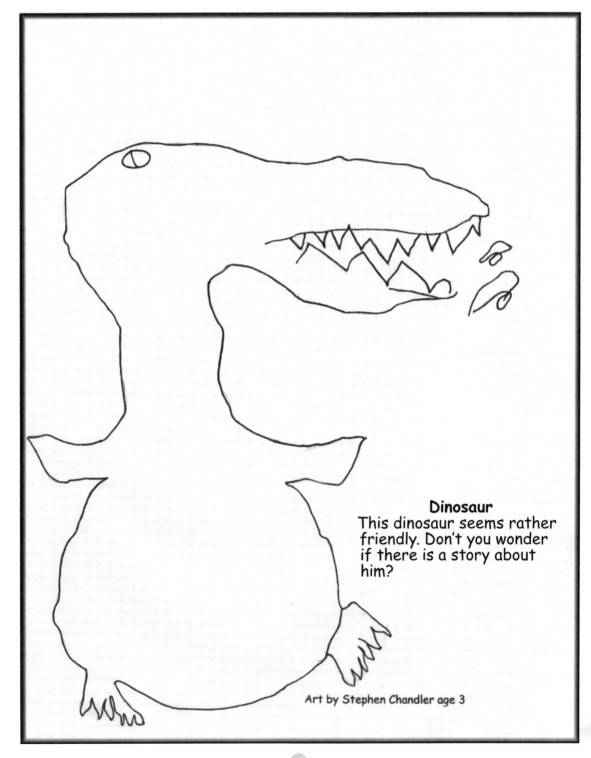

Dinosaur
This dinosaur seems rather friendly. Don't you wonder if there is a story about him?

Art by Stephen Chandler age 3

Chapter 20
THESE ARE TOP SECRETS TO YOUR SUCCESS

You can be a successful storyteller. You may never be rich but you have the ability to define your success. For me **success** is to:

- entertain and delight children.
- present an innovative, fresh storytelling style.
- create opportunities for children to participate in storytelling.
- hold the attention of a group of kids. (That is magic!)
- encourage story writing by adults and children.
- embrace and savor the appreciation I feel when I am storytelling.
- persuade others to tell their stories using some visuals.
- enjoy the delicious *fun of doing it.*

Who is a storyteller?

- ◆ We are **made** of stories… We **are** our stories… We **are all storytellers**.
- ◆ ANYBODY can be a storyteller.
- ◆ *Everybody has a story just waiting to be told.*
- ◆ EVERYONE **is** a storyteller already!
- ◆ Storytellers find a variety of ways to tell a story.
- ◆ Like artists, storytellers create their own style.
- ◆ Everyone teaches and entertains with stories.
- ◆ A storyteller practices diligently to make the story come alive.
- ◆ The storyteller expresses his distinctive perspectives about life.
- ◆ The unique contributions of every culture have been expressed historically through the art of storytelling.

Insights into children…How they benefit from storytelling

- ◆ Children *can* learn things from TV but *they need interaction* with adults, other children, and materials to learn many things. They need to "Do it themselves" to really get it.
- ◆ Young children lack experience and while they are much more knowledgeable than we were at their age, actual experience helps them to understand the story.
- ◆ They need interaction to:
  - develop expressive language
  - increase vocabulary
  - practice thinking
  - develop problem-solving skills
  - use art materials in many ways (which encourages problem-solving)

◆ They have much more receptive (incoming) language than expressive (outgoing) language. This means we must listen to them and provide many chances for them to practice expressive language.

◆ In our culture, children need to be encouraged to relax and have fun using their imaginations.

◆ Have you ever heard a whiny, "I can't see the pictures." No one ever says, "I can't see..." when you're holding a visual on your lap. The beauty of storytelling is that you *can* always see the pictures in your head.

◆ When you don't add visuals or unusual sounds, the audience will be used to seeing the pictures in their heads.

◆ Remind children that they can see the pictures in their heads and they will.

◆ Consider age appropriateness through all aspects of planning, telling and processing stories.

◆ Each child's birth story is different and may be told and retold. The child will never tire of hearing it.

◆ A child may want to sit on your lap. Discourage that if presenting to a group. Feelings are sure to be hurt since they cannot all have a turn to sit on your lap.

◆ Keep in mind who your audience is. They are KIDS, after all, and *kids can equal unpredictability.*

◆ Choose some stories in which kids are smarter than the adults. They always entertain.

◆ Kids won't wait for you to 'get it together.' This makes it quite important to be **very well-prepared**.

◆ Little minds are *busy*! Therefore, stories for groups often have to be shorter than those you might consider reading or telling a child at home

◆ If the audience is very young, the stories must be simple, related to their experience, and short to sustain attention span which plays a big part in how well a story works.

◆ A good teacher always learns more than she teaches and she learns from the children.

Maintaining the listeners' attention

◆ So, how can you make them want to listen?

◆ *A child's attention span grows every day but it still has limits. Children will teach you what those limits are.*

◆ Every age will be able to attend longer with storytelling than with listening to stories being read.

◆ If you have worked with very young children you know that having the child's attention is everything. **It is everything!**

◆ The length of a child's attention span depends upon age, temperament, developmental level, individual interest in the activity, distractions, intelligence, curiosity, and the ability of the adult to maintain the pace of the activity.

◆ Pay attention to wiggles and crabbiness because that is a child's way of telling you that he has reached his limit.

◆ Visuals attract and hold the attention of a child or a group.

◆ ***You can't teach anything if you don't have the child's attention!***

◆ You can grab their attention using your eyes. Look them straight in the eye, especially if they are giving you a problem.

Considerations for choosing stories

◆ You may want to tell a story...

to calm	*to distract*	*to teach concepts*
to delight	*to entertain*	*to promote thought*
to build memories	*to laugh*	*to act silly*

to get in touch with feelings
to consider possibilities
to heighten awareness of feelings and emotions

◆ Look for stories that are unusual or have a surprise element.
◆ Scan your program for stories with topics which might be problematic to particular children. For example, some children have had scary life situations.
◆ Self-image stories are important because they provide encouragement.
◆ Group telling is trickier; what one group loves another finds uninteresting.
◆ When the language is beautiful, the story is enhanced.
◆ Many stories for young children contain repeated lines or repeated actions. These are often described as cumulative stories in that the narrative is added to and all of the lines are repeated with each addition.
◆ When choosing a story for a quilt, consider a simple story with few characters, a well-known story so that omitted details do not detract, and characters that can be easily represented.
◆ "Rhythm and rhyme help people to remember. Rhythm is the sense of movement. Rhymes are words that sound similar. They add to the rhythm, but they also help you remember the next words." Jean Auel *Shelters of Stone*
◆ **The rhythm of the words,** as in Shel Silverstein's *Giraffe and a Half*, may catch your audience.

PRACTICE . . . PRACTICE . . . PRACTICE. BE PREPARED

Mechanics of learning a story

◆ Choosing a story you like is the first step to successful storytelling. It is also a crucial beginning.
◆ Read and re-read the story aloud.
◆ Next, tell and retell the story aloud.
◆ Become aware of the rhythm and feel of the story.
◆ Speak loudly and clearly.
◆ Concentrate on your voice, the words, and the way the story is advanced.
◆ If you are using visual props, practice with those visuals.
◆ Cutting or tearing paper while you tell a story is somewhat like patting your head and rubbing your tummy at the same time. If you are cutting or tearing paper, decide in advance where you will put the scraps.
◆ Memorize some phrases to include in your telling.
◆ Learn a few stories word for word, and be very sure of them before you present them.
◆ Choose a supportive audience and practice telling a story.
◆ Tell a story to a group of children to really "own" it.

PRACTICE . . . PRACTICE . . . PRACTICE. BE PREPARED

Keeping children engaged in storytelling

♦ Know how long it takes to tell each story. Time *your telling, not your reading* of the piece. Pace is different when telling and reading.

♦ Think about whether you should "set up" a story that you suspect is beyond the group's experience. You can do so with a bit of information or conversation.

♦ There is a thread that winds through every story. You must find that thread and follow it to complete a memorable finish.

♦ If your first story should get a less-than-excited response, change the pace.

♦ Children love participation stories, so be sure to learn at least a few of them to include in your storytelling sessions.

♦ Noble qualities (e.g., friendship, responsibility) are best demonstrated through stories that provide a moral. Let the story do its own work in the mind of the child.

♦ Plan at least one active story or movement song like *Who Will Save the Day* to be used if the kids are restless.

♦ If your audience is old enough, you can just tell a story. When you just tell stories, descriptions and details must be colorful and clear.

PRACTICE . . . PRACTICE . . . PRACTICE. BE PREPARED

Approaches to storytelling

Cut, Fold & Tear

◆ Cut, Fold and Tear paper stories are an example of creating attention with the unknown. They tickle the curiosity.

◆ When you are cutting or tearing, paper scraps may drop to the floor. Children will scramble to pick them up. A flat box or small basket held on your lap will catch your scraps and avoid a disturbance.

Chants & Songs

◆ I value using chants and songs with children. While they sing they also *feel the rhythm* and beat of the song and can participate with *their whole body*. A change in pace will allow your performance to continue successfully and may help tame your audience.

Drawn Stories

◆ Drawing is a great attention-getter and sure to entertain. If you keep your drawing simple you will be able to tell and draw at the same time.

Felt Board Stories

◆ Felt board stories have long fascinated children. This old standby is still a very effective way to make a story visible.

◆ Be sure to practice a felt board story at the board with the figures.

Hold On Your Lap Stories

◆ While telling a story, hold a visual on your lap to keep the group's attention.

Participation Stories

◆ Participation stories are simply those stories which anticipate responses or movement by the children. Examples include: slapping your thighs, clapping your hands, pantomiming excitement, pretended puffing up a hill or swimming in a river.

◆ Another type of participation story requires a verbal response. Enlist the help of the audience whenever you give a signal. These stories keep your audience listening carefully for their opportunity to help with the story.

◆ In *My Little Sister Ate One Hare* Little Sister eats quite a variety of strange items. Those things are all added into a basket representing the little girl. As the story ends, scatter the contents of the basket all over the immediate audience. Kids just love this! Look for more stories that lend themselves to this kind of activity.

Quilt Stories

◆ Many stories can be told on quilts. Find a way to both 'quilt a story' and 'tell a quilt'.

◆ Quilts evoke strong feelings of being nurtured. Hold them up for viewing or lay on them, touching the pictures, while telling the story.

◆ Telling a quilt story allows for audience participation and is an excellent opportunity for listeners to use their words.

Story Wheels & Paddle Stories
- Pictures change on a story wheel and keep the group focused on listening to the story.
- Paddle stories allow children to physically participate in a storytelling session.

Visuals
- Visual enhancements are simply surprises on your lap or in your bag.
- Bring out the brown paper bag or a visual and you'll have a group beside you, **listening**.
- You can also do simple origami as you tell a story.

Stories without props
- Stories without significant props hold their own promise of unusual possibilities.
- Repetitious lines, wearing an unusual hat, consulting a long curl of adding machine tape, holding a small pail with a story inside all are gimmicks which lend themselves to many concepts, behavioral issues and funny stories.

General Approaches
- I believe it is much more satisfying to TELL a story than to read it to others.
- Be sure to tell stories more than once so that they become familiar to the children.
- Crazy-Mixed-Up Stories are so much fun! Tell a familiar story...**all wrong!** The audience is sure to object. Once the children feel permission to argue with you they make the give and take very lively.
- If you forget an important part of the story, just stop and say, "Did I forget to tell you...?" (The next time you tell that story they may expect you to say the same thing!)
- Wherever you live, you will be able to locate so-called 'native stories'. They will be valuable to the children you encounter because they often encompass their heritage. Southwest Native American Stories have been included in my collection because of my geographical location.
- **Repetition** (including repeated lines like "I'll huff and I'll puff...") helps the child become part of the story quickly because she anticipates what is to follow.
- Stories with a variety of animals provide the opportunity for the children to make many sounds.
- To check understanding, pay attention to audience behavior.

Moving beyond just telling stories
- Buy and keep the books that become your child's favorites. They will come to cherish them as adults.
- Many stories you tell are stories children don't know. So they wonder, 'What's next? or How will it turn out?'
- Retelling stories is a good activity for children. What comes first? Next? And finally, how does the story end? Story sequence becomes important as children begin to read.
- Some picture books can be sung instead of read. Once you *sing* a story, the children will never let you just read or *tell* it again.
- A carpenter's nail apron decorated to your taste makes a great storyteller's apron. Tied around your waist it is a convenient place for you to hide white board pens, string story cords, folded paper fans for cut paper stories, small scissors, and felt board pieces.

◆ Large Ziplock food storage bags are one effective way to store felt board pieces. For quick retrieval these can be sorted into categories. Storage bags can easily be kept in larger plastic storage containers.

◆ Save your patterns for future use.

◆ The traveling storyteller needs a versatile drawing board, felt board and carrier. The carrier holds it all in one unit which you can sling over your shoulder.

◆ "Make-and-Take It Workshops" are a terrific way to encourage people to begin their own storytelling journeys.

◆ Develop **a basic handout as the skeleton of what you will discuss** during your workshop. Briefly state your ideas about storytelling and **list the titles of stories you have found to be successful**. Lists of stories provide amateurs a place to start. Your handout can serve as a map to guide you through the workshop.

◆ You may enjoy handing out a small evaluation sheet at the end of your session.

◆ You might also consider making up a certificate of attendance.

◆ You will never have all the answers for the questions participants ask, so don't worry about that. In answer you might reply, "I don't know. You'll have to explore that. Let me know what you find out." You might also ask the group for their wisdom related to the question.

◆ Even if you do have an answer they will not always agree with it. Luckily, there is plenty of room for variety of attitude and style in storytelling.

◆ The use of open-ended questions after a good story can create a learning experience. (Note: open-ended questions cannot be answered with yes or no. They demand that the child use expressive language and construct answers using their own words, experiences and observations.)

◆ With the help of a story, the teacher can hook the listeners into considering questions about behavior, feelings, consequences, and possibilities, providing the opportunity to teach concepts.

◆ You have practiced, you have rehearsed. You are ready to begin! Be excited about the story, characters and events.

Writing stories

◆ An important step in the reading process is reading pictures. This happens long before children can read words.

◆ Inventing and writing stories help children understand that words are made up of letters, have meaning, can be put on paper and read, and represent ideas, things, people, feelings and events. The child learns *that she* can arrange words to explain an idea, describe a feeling, or tell a story.

◆ Expect disconnected stories at first. Child development proceeds at a steady pace and little minds march to the beat of the 'developmental drummer'.

◆ When inventing stories with children, remember to ask who, what, when, where, why and how questions. These will cause a story to develop. Ask questions that cannot be answered with 'yes' or 'no'.

- Putting descriptive words together in unique phrases and making comparisons or analogies helps the listener draw mental pictures.
- Scribbling is important as a pleasurable activity, without judgment, that will end in drawing and writing in a few years.
- Create a box of instant story-starters. The children will draw out slips to begin the story, or suggest characters, happenings, or repeated lines.
- As an adult writing stories, there are many triggers you can use to jump-start your creativity. You will find writing your own stories to be a growing experience!

Your evolution as a storyteller?

- At a certain point as a storyteller, you will find yourself bubbling over with new ideas and stories. You might even be asked to do a workshop.
- Consider designing a storyteller business card for yourself.
- Hopefully, the ideas in this book will be a good place for you to start your own storytelling experience. You can expand on existing material and experiment with creating new stories of your own.
- I encourage you to tell or read a story each day.
- Invent your own style of workshop just as you became your own storyteller.
- Jump in, *add to your repertoire or begin your journey as a storyteller. You're sure to have a lot of fun!*
- Keep a list of stories and visuals "in-waiting." Eventually, you will think of how to best utilize these pieces.
- Think of a favorite story and play around with various ideas as you begin to invent your own visuals. It is a creative way to exercise your imagination.
- You ARE a storyteller with an unusual gift to share. Chances are that the children, excited and impressed, will say, "Tell it again!"

People always say to me
"What do you think you'd like to be
When you grow up?"
And I say, "Why,
I think I'd like to be sky
Or be a plane or train or mouse
Or maybe be a haunted house
Or something furry,
rough and wild...
Or maybe I will stay a child."
- Karla Kuskin, Dogs & Dragons, Trees & Dreams

Closing Thoughts...

Storytelling is a passion.
Once you start doing it, you will look at *everything*
as a possible story to tell or as a potential visual for your collection.

Every kind of storytelling has its challenges and its gifts!

Everyone is a STORYTELLER. *Believe it!*

Remember to have fun with it!
You are doing this to charm and entertain children and
your reward will be little faces laughing, surprised and engaged.

Storytelling is addicting.
One small notebook of ideas may one day
grow...
and grow...
and turn into a book.

Whatever you are doing with stories, enjoy yourself!

You have an added advantage over TV or the computer.
You're there! You're alive!
You are present!

So, now that you are at the end of this book...
You may be at the beginning...
of *your own storytelling career.*

I hope you are encouraged to tell many stories.

**I believe that the good student always outdoes
the passionate teacher.**

**Give it your best shot!
I believe in you!
Snip, snap, snout
This tale's told out!**

EVERYONE'S A STORYTELLER

ADULT RESOURCES

Auel, Jean M. *Shelters of Stone.* New York: Crown Publishers, 2002.

Baumgartner, Barbara. *Crocodile! Crocodile! Stories Retold Around the World.* New York: Dorling Kindersley Publishing Inc., 1994.

Baylor, Byrd. *And It Is Still That Way.* Santa Fe, NM: Trails West Publishing, 1988.

Bierhorst, John. *Doctor Coyote.* New York: Mac Millan Publishing Co., 1991.

Bolton, Janet. *Patchwork Folk Art.* New York: Museum Quilt Books, 1995.

Boyd, Ian. *Paper Chains.* USA: Troll, 1997.

Bruchac, Joseph. *Native American Animal Stories.* Golden, CO: Fulcrum Publishing, 1992.

Callaway, Sydney and Gary Witherspoon. *Grandfather Stories of the Navajos.* USA: Curriculum Press, 1974.

Carroll, Louis. *Alice's Adventures in Wonderland.* New York: Random House, 1983.

Cassidy, John and Michael Stroud. *The Klutz Book of Magic.* Palo Alto, CA: Klutz Press, 1990.

Chukovsky, Kornei. *From Two to Five.* Berkley, CA: University of California, 1963.

Collins, Chase. *Tell Me A Story.* Boston, MA: Houghton Mifflin Co., 1992.

Dalt-Weir, Catherine. *Road to Writing: Happily Never After Tangled Tales.* New York: Golden Books, 2000.

Emberley, Ed. *Ed Emberley's Drawing Book of Animals.* New York: Little, Brown & Co., 1970.

— *Ed Emberley's Drawing Book of Birds.* New York: Little, Brown & Co., 1973.

— *Edd Emberley's Drawing Book of Faces.* New York: Little, Brown & Co., 1975.

— *Ed Emberley's Great Thumbprint Drawing Book.* New York: Little, Brown & Co., 1977.

— *Ed Emberley's Picture Pie.* Boston, MA: Little, Brown & Co., 1984.

Fuse, Tomoko. *Simple Traditional Origami.* Tokyo, Japan: Japan Publications, Oriental Trading Co., LTD, 1998.

Goetteman, Joan, Dianne Prentice, Jackie Olmstead, Vicky Ress, Chris Peterson, and Audree Sells. *The Clothesline & Other Quilt Stories.* USA: Six Friends, 2002.

Gorah, Bill. *Fifteen Easy Folk Tales.* New York: Scholastic Books, 1997.

Gray, Dorothy Randall. *Soul Between the Lines.* New York: Avon Books, 1998.

Hayes, Joe. *Here Comes the Storyteller.* El Paso, TX: Cinco Puntos Press, 1996.

— *The Wise Little Burro.* Santa Fe, NM: Trails West Publishing, 1991.

Hoff, Syd. *Drawing Letters and Numbers.* New York: Scholastic, 1993.

Irving, Jan and Robin Currie. *Mudluscious.* Littleton, CO: Libraries Unlimited, 1986.

Jaynes, Caroline F. *String Figures and How to Make Them.* New York: Dover Publications Inc., 1962.

Johnson, Edna, Carrie E. Scott, and Evelyn R. Sickels. *Anthology of Children's Literature, 2nd Edition.* Cambridge, MA: The Riverside Press, 1948.

Kimmel, Eric. *Jar of Fools.* USA: Scholastic Inc., 2000.

Kipling, Rudyard. *How the Alphabet was Made.* New York: Peter Bedrick Books, 1987.

— *How the First Letter was Written.* New York: Peter Bedrick Books, 1987.

Kokaska, Sharen Metz. *Creative Movement for Special Education.* USA: Fearon Publisher, Inc., 1974.

McGuire, Jack. *Creative storytelling: Choosing, Inventing & Sharing Tales for Children.* New York: McGraw Hill Book Co., 1985

Moore, Robin. *Awakening the Hidden Storyteller.* Boston, MA: Shambhala, 1991.

Paley, Vivian Gussin. *The Boy Who Would Be a Helicopter.* Cambridge, MA: Harvard University Press, 1990.

— *Girl with the Brown Crayon.* Cambridge, MA: Harvard University Press, 1997.

— *In Mrs. Tully's Room.* Cambridge, MA: Harvard University Press, 2001.

— *Molly is Three.* Chicago, IL: University of Chicago Press, 1986.

— *Wally's Stories.* Cambridge, MA: Harvard University Press, 1981.

— *White Teacher.* Cambridge, MA: Harvard University Press, 1979.

Pellowski, Anne. *Storyvine.* New York: Mac Millan Publishing Co., 1984.

— *The Family Storytelling Handbook.* New York: Mac Millan Publishing Co., 1987.

Price, Roger. *Droodles.* Los Angeles: Price, Stern, & Sloan, 1981.

Reed, Evelyn Dahl. *Coyote Tales from the Indian Pueblos.* USA: Indian Pueblos, Sunstone Press, 1988.

Rockwell, Anne. *The Three Bears and Other Stories.* New York: Harper and Row, 1975.

Ryder, Joanne. *Earth Dance.* New York: Scholastic, 1996.

Stangl, Jean. *Paper Stories.* USA: Fearon Teaching Aids, Division of David S. Lake, 1981.

Strauss, Susan. *Coyote Stories for Children.* USA: Beyond Words Publishing, 1991.

Supraner, Robyn. *Magic Tricks You Can Do.* Mahwah, NJ: Troll, 1981.

Thompson, Richard. *Draw and Tell.* Toronto, Canada: Annick Press, 1988.

— *The Frog's Riddle: And Other Draw-and-Tell Stories.* Toronto, Canada: Annick Press, 1990.

Trelease, Jim. *The Read-A-Loud-Handbook.* USA: Penguin Books, 2001.

CHILDREN'S PICTURE BOOKS

Asch, Frank. *Bread and Honey.* New York: Parent's Magazine Press, 1981.

— *Sand Cake.* New York: Parent's Magazine Press, 1978.

Ata, Te (Storyteller) and Lynn Moroney. *Baby Rattlesnake.* San Francisco: Children's Press, 1989.

Avery, Kristen. *The Crazy Quilt.* Glenville, IL: Scott, Foresman & Co., 1993.

Aylesworth, Jim. *Old Black Fly.* New York: Scholastic Books, 1992.

Barrett, Judith. *Cloudy with a Chance of Meatballs.* New York: Scholastic Inc., 1978.

Barry, Robert. *Mr. Willowby's Christmas Tree.* New York: McGraw Hill, 1963.

Beifuss, John. *Armadillo Ray.* USA: Troll, 1995.

Birdseye, Tom. *Soap! Soap! Don't Forget the Soap!* New York: Holiday House, 1993.

Bolton, Janet. *Mrs. Noah's Patchwork Quilt.* London, England: Tango Books, 1995.

— *My Grandmother's Patchwork Quilt.* New York: Delecorte Press, 1993.

Bond, Felicia. *Four Valentines in a Rainstorm.* New York: Harper Collins Publishing, 1983.

Briggs, Raymond. *Jim and the Beanstalk.* USA: Putnam, Grosset Group, 1970.

Brown, Jeff. *Flat Stanley.* New York: Scholastic, 1964.

Brown, Margaret Wise. *The Important Book.* USA: Harper & Row, 1949.

Brumbeau, Jeff. *The Quiltmaker's Gift.* Duluth, MN: Pheifer-Hamilton Publishing Co., 2000.

Carle, Eric. *A House for Hermit Crab.* New York: Scholastic, 1992.

— *Draw Me A Star.* New York: Scholastic, 1992.

— *The Mixed-Up Chameleon.* New York: Harper and Row, 1975.

— *Today is Monday.* (Eric Carle Illustrator). New York: Scholastic Books, 1993.

— *The Very Busy Spider.* New York: Putnam & Grosset Group, 1989.

— *Very Hungry Caterpillar.* New York: Philomel, 1994.

Carlson, Nancy. *I Like Me!* USA: Viking Press, 1988.

Charlip, Remy. *Fortunately.* New York: Parents' Magazine Press, 1964.

Cohen, Caron Kee. *Whiffle Squeak.* USA: Puffin Books, 1987.

Crockett, Johnson. *Harold and the Purple Crayon.* New York: Scholastic Book Services, 1970.

Cronin, Doreen. *Click, Clack, Moo Cows That Type.* New York: Simon & Schuster, 2000.

Eastman, P. D. *Are You My Mother?* New York: Random House Beginner Books, 1960.

Edwards, Pat. *A Big Fat Pie.* Essex, England: Longman Group, 1987.

Fleischman, Paul. *Lost! A Story in String.* New York: Henry Holt & Co., 2000.

Gackenbach, Dick. *Claude the Dog.* New York: Clarion Books, 1974.

Galdone, Paul. *The Greedy Old Fat Man.* New York: Clarion Books, 1983.

Garfield, Valerie. *Harold and the Purple Crayon: The Birthday Present.* USA: Harper Collins, 2002.

Gilman, Phoebe. *Something From Nothing.* New York: Scholastic Inc., 1992.

Graham, Bob. *The Red Woolen Blanket.* Cambridge, MA: Blackbird Design, 1987.

Grossman, Bill. *My Little Sister Ate One Hare.* New York: Scholastic, 1996.

Guback, Georgia. *Luka's Quilt.* New York: William Morrow & Co., Greenwillow Books, 1994.

Hayes, Joe. *No Way José.* Santa Fe, NM: Trails West Publishing, 1986.

— *The Wise Little Burro.* Sante Fe, NM: Trails West Publishing, 1991.

Heine, Helme. *The Most Wonderful Egg in the World.* USA: Aladdin Books, 1987.

Hoberman, Mary Akin (Adapted by). *Miss Mary Mack.* USA: Scholastic Inc., 1998.

Hooper, Meredith. *Seven Eggs.* Hong Kong: Harper Collins, 1985.

Hopkinson, Deborah. *Sweet Clara and the Freedom Quilt.* New York: Alfred Knopf, 1993.

Hurd, Thatcher. *Mama Don't Allow.* USA: Harper Trophy, 1984.

Hutchins, Pat. *Don't Forget the Bacon.* New York: Scholastic, 1995.

— *The Doorbell Rang.* New York: Greenwillow Books, 1986.

Jackson, Alison. *I Know An Old Lady Who Swallowed a Pie.* New York: Scholastic Inc., 1997.

Jackson, Kathryn B. *Animals' Merry Christmas.* New York: Golden Press, 1974.

Johnston, Tony. *Five Little Foxes in the Snow.* New York: Harper and Row Publishers, 1977.

— *Quilt Story.* New York: G. P. Putnam, 1985.

Katz, Alan. *Take Me Out of the Bathtub.* New York: Simon & Schuster Children's Books, 2001.

Kent, Jack. *Joey.* New York: Scholastic Book Services, 1985.

Kimmel, Eric. *I Took My Frog to the Library.* USA: Penguin Group, 1990.

Kipling, Rudyard. *Just So Stories.* New York: Peter Bedrick Books, 1987.

Kirn, Ann. *Nine in a Line.* New York: W. W. Norton & Co., 1966.

Krauss, Ruth. *The Carrot Seed.* New York: Scholastic Book Services, 1966.

Lionni, Leo. *Little Blue, Little Yellow.* United States: Mulberry Paperback, 1995.

— *Six Crows.* New York: Scholastic Books, 1995.

— *Swimmy.* New York: Scholastic Inc., 1989.

Lobel, Arnold. *Frog and Toad Are Friends.* New York: Harper Trophy, 1970.

Longfellow, Henry Wadsworth. *Hiawatha.* New York: Penguin Putnam, 1996. Susan Jeffers, Illustrator.

Martin, Bill. *Brown Bear, Brown Bear, What Do You See?* New York: Henry Holt and Co. Inc., 1996.

Martinez, Estefania. *The Naughty Little Rabbit and Old Man Coyote.* Chicago: Children's Press, 1992.

McGovern, Ann. *Too Much Noise.* New York: Houghton Mifflin Company 1987.

McKee, David. *Elmer.* New York: Lothrop, Lee & Shepard Books, 1968.

McPhail, David. *Drawing Lessons From A Bear.* New York: Little & Brown Co., 2000.

Merriam, Eve. *Train Leaves the Station.* New York: Bill Martin Books, Henry Holt, 1988.

Mills, Lauren. *The Rag Coat.* New York: Little, Brown & Co., 1991.

Milne, A. A. *Winnie the Pooh.* New York: E. P. Dutton, 1988.

Moore, Clement C. *The Night Before Christmas.* New York: Golden Press, 1976.

Most, Bernard. *Z-Z-Zoink!* San Diego, CA: Harcourt Brace & Company, 1999.

Munsch, Robert. *Alligator Baby.* New York: Scholastic, 1977.

— *Thomas' Snowsuit.* Toronto, Canada: Annick Press, 1989.

Numeroff, Laura Joffe. *If You Give A Mouse A Cookie.* New York: Scholastic Books, 1985.

Polacco, Patricia. *The Keeping Quilt.* New York: Simon & Schuster, 1988.

— *Oh, Look!* New York: Philomel Books, 2004.

Prelutsky, Jack. *A Pizza the Size of the Sun.* New York: Scholastic Books, 1994.

Rafe, Martin. *Foolish Rabbit's Big Mistake.* New York: G. P. Putnam, 1985.

Rathman, Peggy. *Good Night, Gorilla.* New York: G. P. Putnam & Sons, 1994.

Rosen, Michael. *Mission Ziffoid.* Cambridge, MA: Candlewick Press, 1999.

Seuss, Dr. *Horton Hatches the Egg.* New York: Random House, 1968.

Shulman, Lisa. *Old Mac Donald Had a Woodshop.* New York: G. P. Putnam & Son, 2002.

Slepian, Jan and Ann Seidler. *The Hungry Thing.* USA: Scholastic Book Services, 1971.

Shannon, George. *Lizard's Song.* New York: Greenwillow Books, 1981.

Sharmat, Marjorie Weinman. *A Big Fat Enormous Lie.* New York: E. P. Dutton, 1978.

Shaw, Charles G. *It Looked Like Spilt Milk.* New York: Harper & Row, 1947.

Silverstein, Shel. *Giraffe and a Half.* New York: Harper & Row, 1964.

Slobodkina, Esphyr. *Caps for Sale.* New York: Harper Trophy, 1940.

Steig, William. *Pete's A Pizza.* USA: Harper Collins Publishers, 1998.

— *Sylvester and the Magic Pebble.* New York: Simon Schuster, 1969.

Stevenson, James. *Don't Make Me Laugh.* Singapore: Farrar, Straus and Giroux, 1999.

Tenorio-Coscarelli, Jane. *Piñata Quilt.* Murieta, CA: 1/4 Inch Designs & Publishing Co., 1999.

— Jane. *Tamale Quilt.* Murieta, CA: 1/4 Inch Designs & Publishing Co., 1999.

— Jane. *Tortilla Quilt.* Murieta, CA: 1/4 Inch Designs & Publishing Co., 1999.

Thurber, James. *Many Moons.* USA: Harper, Brace, Jovanovich Publishing Co., 1943.

Tresselt, Alvin. *The Mitten.* USA: Scholastic Inc., 1964.

Van Allsburg, Chris. *Polar Express.* New York: Houghton Mifflin, 1985.

Van Laan, Nancy. *Possum Come A-Knockin'.* New York: Al Knopf-Dragonfly Books, 1990.

Vaughan, Marcia. *Wombat Stew.* New York: Silver Burdett, 1984.

Waterstone, Rachel. *Who's Under Grandma's Quilt?* Clarksville, TN: First Story Press, 1997.

West, Judy. *Have You Got My Purr?* New York: Dutton's Children's Books, 1999.

Westcott, Nadine Bernard. *The Lady With the Alligator Purse.* Boston, MA: Little, Brown & Co., 1988.

Willard, Nancy. *Simple Pictures Are Best.* New York: Scholastic Inc., 1994.

Williams, Linda. *Little Old Lady Who Was Not Afraid of Anything.* New York: Harper, 1986.

Williams, Sue. *I Went Walking.* San Diego, CA: Harcourt Brace, 1989.

Wyllie, Stephen. *There Was an Old Woman.* New York: Harper and Row Publishing, 1985.

Ziefert, Harriet and Mavis Smith. *Going On A Lion Hunt.* New York: Viking Penguin Inc., 1989.

TRADITIONAL TALES AND RHYMES

Bremen Town Musicians (Jacob & Wilhelm Grimm, German Folk Tale)
Chicken Little [Henny Penny] (English Folk Tale)
The Emperor's New Clothes (Hans Christian Andersen 1837)
Fly Away Jack, Fly Away Jill (Rhyme)
The Gingerbread Boy (English Folk Tale)
Goldilocks and the Three Bears (English Folk Tale)
The House that Jack Built (English Folk Tale)
Jack and the Beanstalk (English Folk Tale)
Little Red Riding Hood (Jacob and Wilhelm Grimm, German Folk Tale)
The Old Woman and Her Pig (English Folk Tale)
One Elephant Went Out to Play (Singing Game)
The Three Billy Goats Gruff (Scandinavian Folk Tale)
The Story of the Three Little Pigs (English Folk Tale)

EVERYONE'S A STORYTELLER